To all those who share my love of food.

Acknowledgments

I am most grateful to all who have helped in the production of this book. Many friends have given valuable advice and time, without which this project would never have materialised. I would like to thank in particular, David, Amy, Stewart, Clare, Jess, Kate and Mike.

As always, I would like to thank my parents for their continued support and enthusiasm.

Special thanks to Sophie Sitwell who has worked extremely hard in taking the superb photographs and providing the illustrations. I am also indebted to Denis Sitwell who has been the model for this book. Having been subjected to wearing a tea pot on his head and other peculiar poses all in the name of art, I owe him many thanks.

MAN ABOUT THE KITCHEN

The Novice's Guide To
Cookery for Men

ALASTAIR WILLIAMS

SUMMERSDALE

Summersdale Publishers
46 West Street
Chichester
West Sussex
PO19 1RP
United Kingdom

A CIP catalogue record for this book is available from the British Library.

Printed and bound in Great Britain
by Selwood Printing Ltd., Burgess Hill.

Cover design, illustrations and photography by the multi-talented Sophie Sitwell.

CONTENTS

Start Here . . .

If this book has been bought for you in the hope of encouraging you towards the kitchen, other than to retrieve a cool beer or ice for a gin and tonic, I trust that you will take the time to read it. You might be pleasantly surprised to discover a world beyond microwave meals and fish and chips. There is a chance that you have bought this book for yourself because you have a desire to learn how to cook. Or maybe you've got a hot date with the most beautiful girl in town and all you can cook is fish fingers with chilli sauce. Perhaps your wife has given you an ultimatum - either you start to help with the cooking or you wash your own smalls. The book won't guarantee that you get your girl or manage to hold onto the one you've got, but it will teach you how to cook!

There are an awful lot of men out there who are struggling to get through the burger and baked bean barrier. Fear not, help is at hand. Although this book will not turn you into the next 'super chef', it will teach you how to cook a variety of meals ranging from simple dishes, such as scrambled eggs, to others that are more elaborate.

Cooking is regarded by many as a chore, its purpose being purely to sustain life with as little effort as possible. Perhaps you rarely cook for yourself, preferring to rely on others or on take-aways or ready-to-cook meals. If you are one such person then it's time to change. Being able to cook is not solely a useful social skill. It should provide enjoyment and entertainment. Not only is it nice to cook for a partner, it is something that can be enjoyed together. Another benefit from being able to cook is that it might get you out of the washing-up if you have prepared a meal.

As you learn more about cooking you will begin to learn more about food. Most chefs are as passionate about the ingredients as they are about cooking, inferior ingredients will normally result in an inferior meal. Cooking combines creativity, skill, timing and knowledge plus at the end of it you can eat what you have created, which is one up on an oil painting! You might not give a stuff about how it looks provided it tastes good and there is plenty of it; each to their own. The intent of this book is simply to get you cooking, not to preach about etiquette and cuisine politics.

After a little use, you will notice the heavy influence of French Cuisine upon this book. There is a particular bias of cooking from the Provençal region, where I have spent a great deal of

7

time over the last 13 years. I have been fortunate enough to meet people who share my passion for food and who have taken the trouble to impart knowledge, enthusiasm and guidance on many of the famous dishes from the region. There is always something new to learn, and I continue my quest with an open mind and an open mouth prepared for my next culinary adventure.

The Rudiments

Being a good cook does not mean that you have to be able to create dazzling masterpieces every time you enter a kitchen. Learning how to cook is a gradual process that takes time and patience. Even the most experienced chefs have disasters. Remember that cooking is an art not a science. You will find that even when you follow a recipe word for word it does not always turn out the way it should. I am not trying to shift the blame from any of the recipes that are in this book, but there are many factors that affect the final result and you have to be aware of this. If you repeat a recipe several times over it is unlikely that it will ever taste or look exactly the same. With experience you will learn how to adapt recipes to your own tastes and skills.

One of the best ways of improving your cooking is to watch other cooks. This is where you pick up the little tricks and secrets that will enable you to increase your knowledge and skill. It is sensible to keep a small notebook so that you can jot down ideas and tips that you come across. Half the fun of cooking is in experimenting, using old skills and recipes and combining them with new ideas.

Kitchen Equipment

Any craftsman will have a set of tools that is essential to his trade. The same principle applies to the cook. There is a plethora of gadgets and gizmos on the market for cooks. It is very easy to believe that they are all essential, it is only when you see your cupboards bursting with juicers, sandwich makers, blenders, steamers, yoghurt makers etc that you realise you have little room left for the food. Although some gadgets can aid the chef - speeding up laborious tasks such as grating cheese - others are dispensable and will soon find their way to the back of the cupboard after the novelty has worn off. As a rule, it is far better to buy a few quality items than a number of inferior products. A frying pan that bends under the weight of a couple of sausages is going to be useless. Quality in cooking equipment often equates to weight, a pan should have a thick bottom and a sturdy handle. However this does not mean that if you find a saucepan that is so heavy that you need to start body-building before you can pick it up, it is necessarily going to be the best.

Kitchen Knives

Investing in a quality set of knives is essential. Very few people have adequate kitchen knives, often relying on blunt flimsy instruments that are potentially dangerous. When choosing knives bear in mind for which job they are intended. It is sensible to have a selection of different sizes; it being difficult to use a 10 inch blade for peeling fruit. I generally use just two sizes, a small cook's knife with a 3 inch blade, and a large 7 inch knife. It is also useful to have a serrated knife for cutting fruit. If you have the choice between buying a cheap set of knives and a couple of high quality knives, go for the latter.

The Freezer

The main advantage of having a freezer is that large quantities of food can be stored and used as and when required. If you arrive home late and are feeling too tired to cook then it is a joy to be able to go to the freezer and take out a ready-prepared meal. They can also save you time and money as food can be prepared and bought in bulk. When cooking a pasta sauce why not make double the amount, and freeze what is unused? A freezer is also useful for storing seasonal fruit and vegetables, so you can enjoy them any time of year.

To aid fast freezing do not place large quantities of unfrozen food into the freezer at one go. This raises the temperature of the freezer and slows down the freezing process. Furthermore, food that has been cooked should be cold before being placed in the freezer.

If you are low on food or have an unexpected guest then there should hopefully be something in the freezer that you can use. This is where the problem begins: do you know what is in your freezer and, perhaps more importantly, how long it has been there? It amazes me how many people's freezer contents lack any type of a labelling. It is either a case of lucky dip or trying to feel what is wrapped up, which is no easy task when the items are frozen. I have heard these mystery items referred to as UFO's (unidentified frozen objects).

So it is essential that your freezer is organised: this will save you time and money.

● Label and date all the items in your freezer. It is also a good idea to keep a separate list on the outside of the freezer door which you can update every time you add or remove something.

• Freezers run more efficiently when they are full, so try to keep your freezer well stocked even if it is half full of bread.

If you are going to make full use of your freezer then it is worth investing in a specific book that provides information on the different methods of preparing food for the freezer as well as telling you what can be frozen and for how long. Don't think that just because it is frozen you can retrieve a steak and kidney pie that your mother made for you in 1979.

Sensibility

Cooking combines a number of senses, with influences from both artistic and scientific domains. There is also the element of common sense. The recipes in this book are created with simplicity in mind, both in terms of implements and cooking skills required. However an element of common sense enters into the equation as I don't want to be held responsible for a person who ends up in the hospital burns department for having misunderstood the instruction "stand in boiling water for 20 minutes".

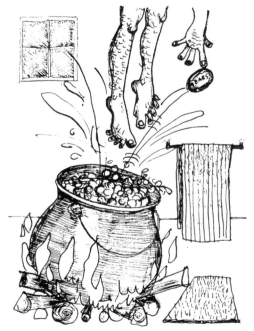

Another important point to remember is that all cooking times and temperatures are approximate. Not all ovens will take the same amount of time to cook a meal. If, for example, it is fan assisted you will have to allow for the extra efficiency. Cooking is ultimately intuitive and no amount of instructions can replace this. Before you try any recipe read through it first to make sure you have the ingredients and the time to prepare it.

The Kitchen

Just as a well organised garage has a wide selection of high quality tools and adequate working space, the same applies to the kitchen. The purpose of a kitchen is to prepare food, therefore the element of hygiene must not be ignored. If you are a bachelor then it is perfectly understandable to want to show your independence by being as messy as possible. However once you reach the stage of the overflowing bin surrounded by empty take-away boxes you know it is time to consider clearing up.

Although we usually have better things to do than worry about such trivialities as cleaning, I had better try to advocate virtuous behaviour, lest I become a target for irate girlfriends, wives and mothers. So to keep everyone happy good kitchen practice is to be recommended.

The three main areas are organisation, safety, and hygiene.

Organisation and Safety:

- Keep heavy items in the lower cupboards.

- Never use a stool to stand on whilst trying to reach an object. Even a chair can be unstable. So ideally you should have a small kitchen step ladder.

- The kitchen should be well ventilated so fumes and heat are removed quickly.

- There should be plenty of light, natural or artificial.

- Fire blanket and extinguisher should be kept handy.

- Keep cupboards tidy.

- Take care with the positioning of pans on your cooker. Remember to keep the handles from protruding over the edge of the cooker.

- Make sure that handles on pots and pans are not loose.

- Keep an eye out for damaged flexes on electrical appliances such as toasters and kettles.

- Use caution when using electrical gadgets such as blenders and food processors.

- Keep matches and sharp knives out of reach from children.

- Knives should be kept sharp, as a blunt knife can slip when cutting and cause an accident.

- Kitchen knives should be kept in a knife block. Keeping them in a drawer not only causes the knives to lose their sharpness, it also makes it too easy to cut oneself.

- Never learn to juggle using kitchen knives. Old socks filled with rice make a safer alternative. Any type of rice will do, except egg-fried rice.

Fat Fires:

If you should experience a pan of fat igniting then remain calm and follow these rules.

- Never throw water on top of the oil - this will make it worse.

- Turn off the gas or electric hob if you can safely do so, otherwise wait until the fire has been extinguished.

- The most effective way to put out a fat fire is to get a dampened tea towel and place it over the top of the pan. Do not remove it for at least five minutes after the flames have subsided.

- If the fire is out of control, call the fire brigade and leave the house.

If you have children make sure they understand the kitchen is not an extension of the playground. I was once working in a restaurant and during one of the last few days before Christmas we had a family come in for lunch. The mother asked if we could look after her seven year old son whilst she finished her shopping. It was an unusual request, but she seemed desperate saying that she found it impossible to shop with her son. Begrudgingly we said 'yes', and she departed hastily. It was no wonder the mother left him with us, he was a monster, creating chaos within seconds. He made his way into the kitchen, where he started prodding and trying to eat a variety of foods. By this stage we had realised that he was uncontrollable and his parents had probably left for South America. The child then made a big mistake: seeing a bowl of dried hot chillies he inquired as to what they were. We told him and said that he definitely did not want to eat them. Naturally, therefore, he picked up a number of dried chillies and put them in his mouth before we could stop him. I thought he was going to explode, his eyes were like a couple of waterfalls and he ran around screaming for about half an hour. Eventually the parents returned to pick up the little brat. I think he learnt his lesson. We learnt never to look after children unless a bowl of chilli peppers is to hand!

Hygiene
Not wishing to get into the gory details, being violently sick is usually a consequence of bad hygiene. Harmful bacteria can spread quickly in the right conditions, so here are a few guide-lines.

- All surfaces such as worktops, floors and cookers should
be cleaned regularly, preferably every day.

- Never let your kitchen surfaces get cluttered. Clean up as
you go along. This makes food preparation easier as well
as reducing the burden of cleaning at the end of the process.
Let's face it no one likes washing up, but it has to be done.
I know the old excuse "I did the cooking, so someone else
can do the washing up" is a good trick, but a good chef
always clears up after himself. I can't remember his name,
though.

- Clean the door seals on fridges and freezers on a regular
basis.

- Keep cooking utensils clean.

- Don't leave meat or fish out of the fridge for any lengthy period, especially if it has been cooked.

- Throw away food that passed its 'use by' date.

- Wash all fruit and vegetables.

- Make sure meat is sufficiently cooked. If you are having your meat rare, it must be as fresh as possible.

- Allow large pieces of frozen meat to defrost completely before cooking.

You Want Me To Do What?

Although some cooking terms might seem obvious there are probably many of you out there who will have trouble even finding the kitchen, let alone understanding recipe instructions.

Baste
To spoon fat or oil over food, in order to keep it moist. Usually done to a joint of meat intermittently during its roasting.

Beat
This is the mixing of ingredients using a wooden spoon, a fork or a whisk.

Chop
To cut into small pieces.

Cream
To mix fat with a another ingredient such as sugar until it becomes creamy.

Dice
To cut into small cubes.

Grate
A grater can produce coarse or fine shavings of food, such as cheese or vegetables.

Knead
To use your knuckles to smooth dough out, the idea being to create a smooth texture.

Marinade
A combination of juices, spices, or oils, in which meat is soaked to enhance the flavour.

Parboil
This is the partial boiling of something. The cooking will then normally be completed by another method. This applies, for example, to roast potatoes.

Peel
To the remove the skin or the outer layer of a vegetable or fruit.

Rub in
To rub flour and fat together between your fingertips until it resembles breadcrumbs.

Simmer

To cook just below boiling point, so that only an occasional bubble appears on the surface.

Order a Take-away

To telephone for a pizza when your cooking goes disastrously wrong.

Weights And Measures

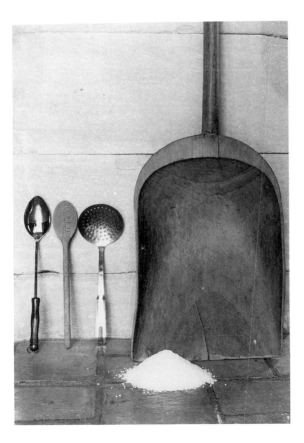

There are certain things that indicate our age. Comments such as 'during the war' and 'I remember when you got a couple of lamb chops for a shilling', or alternatively when someone asks you what you think of Take That, and you say, 'take who?', are pointers as to our age. You might be asking 'what do a teen pop band, a couple of lamb chops and 'The War' have to do with food?' Well not a lot, but somewhere in the mists of time the country went metric. Those Imperial days are now long gone, but many people still prefer to think in Imperial weights and measures, as I do myself. Hence the need to be able to convert Metric to Imperial and vice versa. Other amounts are referred to in spoons or cups which are self-explanatory.

The following abbreviations are used:

Tbs = Tablespoon
Tsp = Teaspoon

If you don't possess a set of kitchen weighing scales then it is possible to convert certain ingredients into spoon measures. Obviously the weights of all ingredients will vary, but here are some rough measures...

1 Tbs = 1 oz (25g) of...syrup, jam, honey etc
2 Tbs = 1 oz (25g) of...butter, margarine, lard, sugar
3 Tbs = 1 oz (25g) of...cornflour, cocoa, custard powder, flour
4 Tbs = 1 oz (25g) of...grated cheese, porridge oats

All spoon measures refer to level spoons, not heaped.

1 tsp (teaspoon) = 5ml
1 tbs (tablespoon) = 15 ml

1 mug of rice weighs roughly 8 oz (225g)

The approximations used for conversion between Metric and Imperial in this book are as follows...

1 oz = 25g
2 oz = 50g
3 oz = 75g
4 oz = 100g
6 oz = 150g
8 oz = 225g
1 lb = 500g

1/4 pint = 150ml
1/2 pint = 300ml
1 pint = 600ml
2 pints = 1 litre

Gas Mark	Deg C	Deg F
1	140	275
2	150	300
3	170	325
4	180	350
5	200	400
6	225	425
7	230	450
8	240	475
9	250	500

Healthy Eating

Healthy eating has been in vogue for a while now. Fads change almost as frequently as the boffins change their minds as to what we should and should not be eating. There is increasing pressure to adopt a healthier lifestyle, take regular exercise and cut down on fatty foods (sounds like torture). Healthy eating is something that many of us pay little thought to - decadence is more fun, after all. But if your idea of a balanced diet means equal amounts of food to alcohol, you should read this section.

As the old saying goes 'we are what we eat': if you eat a lot of lard you tend to look like it. Aside from the aesthetics, heart disease, high blood pressure and numerous other illnesses are linked to poor eating habits.

In general a diet should be low in fat, cholesterol and salt, with a regular intake of the necessary vitamins.

If you want to stay healthy you must have a balanced diet. There are certain elements that are essential to achieve this.

Carbohydrates
These are the providers of energy and can be found predominantly in fruits, vegetables and grains.

Fats
We are constantly being reminded that we shouldn't be fat, for both health and aesthetic reasons. However it is not easy to do something about it. If you are confused by all the talk about different types of fats I will enlighten you. There are two basic types; saturated and unsaturated. The saturated fats are divided into polyunsaturated fats and monounsaturated fats. The term 'fat' as we know it, usually refers to a substance of both poly and monounsaturated fats. It is the saturated fats that are detrimental to our health. Too much saturated fat can increase the likelihood of heart disease as the arteries become clogged, thus impeding the blood supply.

Although we should not overdo fat intake we cannot do without it. Fat is an important source of energy for the body, but fats take longer to digest than carbohydrates. This means fat is useful for storing energy. It is present in a variety of products such as butter, margarine, milk, cheese and of course, meat.

By looking at the fat content on packaging you can see how much you are consuming. Low fat versions of many products are now available, although there is a tendency to regard them as an inferior substitute to the 'real thing'. More often than not it is a psychological mechanism trying to tell us that they don't taste as good.

Proteins

They are referred to as the 'building blocks' of the body. Proteins are produced from a combination of amino acids and are found in fish, lean meat, milk, cheese and eggs. Proteins are used to regenerate vital hormones such as insulin, adrenalin and thyroxin. A shortage of proteins results in poor growth or poor development of body cells.

Vitamins

This is one area where many people fail to supply their bodies correctly. The following are the most essential vitamins and their sources along with some of the maladies that are incurred as consequence of the vitamin's absence.

Vitamin A

Vitamin A is present in dairy products such as cheese, butter and milk as well as in green vegetables and liver. It is needed for growth, and resistance against disease.

Vitamin B

Vitamin B is not one vitamin but a complex consisting of more than 16 different vitamins. They are to be found in whole grain cereals, liver, yeast, and lean meat.

Vitamin C

The main source of the vitamin is citrus fruits (for example lemons, oranges, and blackcurrants) and fresh vegetables. Vitamin C is needed for the efficient functioning of the brain and nervous system. It also increases our immune response to infectious diseases including the common cold.

Vitamin D
A deficiency in calcium can lead to weak and brittle bones, a condition known as Rickets, which predominantly affects children. In adults it can result in bow-legs. Thankfully vitamin D deficiency is a rarity now in this country. Vitamin D is found in milk, butter, cheese, oily fish and liver.

Vitamin E
This is a vitamin that does not usually pose a deficiency problem in our society. It is found in milk, cheese, butter and meat. One of vitamin E's most important functions is that it helps to keep the blood from coagulating, thus preventing internal blood clots.

Vitamin K
This is found in green vegetables. It helps the blood clotting process, which is useful after a cut.

Roughage
This is vital if you want to keep all your passages open, or if you are having trouble making substantial deposits. High fibre cereals provide a good source of roughage.

Water
It may seem obvious that the body requires a substantial amount of water in order to function correctly, but take this as a friendly reminder.

Minerals
There are three main minerals whose continued supply can all too easily be jeopardised: iron, calcium and iodine. Other

minerals such as the phosphates, potassium, magnesium and sodium are generally in good supply.

Iron

This is vital for the formation of the red blood cells. If a person has a deficiency of iron it can lead to anaemia. This is a shortage of red blood cells. Women find they are more prone to this than men. Ensuring a high iron intake is not as simple as eating a bag of nails, however. Far better to eat liver, which is slightly more palatable, and is an excellent source of iron, as are other meats.

Calcium

This mineral is important for strong bones and teeth. It is found in dairy products.

Iodine

Iodine, although important, is not needed in the same quantities as calcium or iron. Fish is a good source of iodine.

Minerals and vitamins are available in pills from health food shops and supermarkets. Some contain multi vitamins, while others are more specific. It is still important to follow the recommended dosage.

Losing Weight

"Hold on" you are thinking, "is this a book for men or what? Real men don't diet, a man's belly is a symbol of his capacity for large volumes of drink and food and is nothing to be ashamed of." The only problem is that when you go on holiday and are sitting on the beach surrounded by bronzed

Adonis's you and your belly might look a little out of place, so it's wise to keep that T-shirt on!

There is always some new wonder diet that promises to help you lose weight. Women's magazines are constantly running features on how to lose weight, and the diet industry as a whole is worth millions. All I am going to say on this delicate matter is that disciplined, sensible and regular eating is one of the most effective ways of reducing weight. It has been shown that after dieting most people put the weight back on in the long term. Therefore it is much more sensible to take a look at what you normally eat and see if there are certain components that can be cut out; fried pies or bread and dripping are best avoided.

If you do want to try to lose some weight here are a few tips.

- Set a realistic target. Don't cut out all chocolate instantly: reduce your intake to just bars after each meal, and a few weeks later bring it down to 2 and so on.

- Don't expect to lose weight straight away or at a consistent rate.

- Be strict with yourself.

- Don't give up. Not yet, anyway.

The Store Cupboard

With 24 hour garages now stocking a wide range of food, as long as you live near one you are never going to be short of food. They seem to stock everything from dog food to frozen Mars bars, not that you would want to eat a tin of Bonzo's Beef with a Mars bar.

A well-stocked store cupboard is essential for any cook as the garage does have certain limitations. Although a certain degree of improvisation is possible there are a number of basic ingredients that should always be kept in stock. It is a common problem when cooking that whatever ingredients you have in your cupboard will always be the things you don't need, while whatever you do need will be conspicuous by its absence.

There are certain items that you will find that you use constantly, such as tinned tomatoes, pasta, rice, cheese. Make sure that you keep an adequate supply of these basic items. You will also need a variety of spices and herbs.

Oils and Vinegars

Buying habits have become much more exotic and sophisticated over the last few decades. Foreign travel has meant that people are more likely to experience food from different countries and cultures. People also appear to have become more adventurous with what they eat. Where it would have once been impossible to find exotic foreign ingredients, such as baby sweetcorn or mange tout, they are now regarded as everyday products and are found in most supermarkets. The increased prevalence of such variety has meant that it is relatively easy to create authentic foreign cuisine.

In cooking there are a variety of oils that can be used. The most frequently used are blended vegetable oil, sunflower oil, corn oil and olive oil. Each of the oils is very different in flavour so experiment with each type to see which flavour you prefer. There is no doubt that the most highly prized of those oils is olive oil. Olive oil experts are a little like wine experts: they can tell by taste the origin of a particular oil, be it Shell, Castrol or plain 3-in-1. The majority of the olive oil we use comes from France, Italy, Spain or Greece. The oil is produced by the pressing of the olives. The first cold pressing produces the best quality oil which is called Extra Virgin Olive Oil. The olives are then pressed again to produce a lower quality oil and a corresponding price. Olive oil is not the sort of oil in which you would fry chips, it is expensive and inappropriately flavoured. However olive oil can't be beaten for French dressings, mayonnaise or cooking small cuts of meat. Other more unusual oils include walnut oil which can be used in salads to add a nutty flavour, or Sesame seed oil which is used in Chinese cuisine.

Vegetables

Nutritionists are right when they say that we should increase the proportion of vegetables in our diets. Unless we're vegetarian. Many people seem to have an adversity to anything that is healthy or fresh. In the past the supply of vegetables was usually determined by what was available locally according to season, supermarkets are now vegetable havens all year round, with exotic vegetables from the Far East alongside local produce. Although many of these imports are not cheap they do add tremendous variety.

There is still a tendency for people to over-cook vegetables, which for me always conjures a picture of school meals that would rather be forgotten. If you are cooking vegetables remember to measure their cooking time, don't leave them indefinitely. Vegetables taste and look better when cooked correctly and they retain more of their nutritional value.

Below is a list of some of the common and not-so-common vegetables currently available, explaining how they should be prepared and various methods of cooking.

Artichokes (Globe)

They are interesting vegetables in terms of shape and texture. If you are buying artichokes make sure they look and feel fresh with no brown tinges to the leaves, if the leaves are drying out leave them.

Before cooking remove a few of the tough outer leaves, cut off the stalks, and then wash. Place in a pan of salted boiling water, reduce the heat to a simmer and continue to simmer until an outside leaf can be removed with ease. This should take about 30 minutes, depending on the size and age of the artichoke.

Drain well and serve. Remove the tough outer leaves to expose the tender ones. Dip in melted butter, then eat the fleshy part of the leaf discarding the rest. The treasured piece of the artichoke is the heart which is found at the bottom of the leaves. Do not eat the fluffy centre as it has an unpleasant taste.

As an alternative serve them cold with a Vinaigrette dressing.

Asparagus

This is not your everyday vegetable, but it is well worth splashing out on once in a while. Try to use asparagus as soon it is bought, don't keep it for days. When buying asparagus pick bundles that contain heads of the same size.

Untie the bundles. Remove about one to two inches off the stalk. Using a small knife scrape downwards to remove the outer layer. Wash and tie back into bundles. Place the asparagus in a deep pan and simmer for about 10 minutes or until tender. Serve straight away with either butter, mayonnaise or Hollandaise sauce.

Aubergine/Eggplant

There are a number of varieties, but the most common are purple in colour. When buying aubergine choose those with a firm skin. Cut the top and bottom off and then slice thinly. Before cooking it is normal to extract the bitter juice that is present. Sprinkle lightly with salt and leave for 20 minutes. Before cooking, rinse the slices in water, then pat dry with a paper towel. The usual method for cooking aubergines is to fry them either in oil or butter until they soften.

Baby Sweetcorn

This expensive import from the Orient is worth the price. The only preparation needed is washing, (don't forget behind your ears), following which they can be gently boiled or fried. To benefit from their full flavour they need to retain their crispness, so don't over-cook.

Beans - French

Wash them and top and tail. Cut into 1 inch lengths, or leave whole. To cook, place in boiling salted water and cook for 10 to 15 minutes. After cooking they can be tossed in butter.

Broccoli

Wash in cold water. Cut off the stalks then divide into flowerets (clumps). Place in boiling water for about 10 minutes. Don't over-cook as it will cause the broccoli to become mushy losing most of its flavour and colour.

Brussels Sprouts

If there was one vegetable that was always over-cooked at school it was the sprout. In those halcyon days you weren't allowed to leave the table until you had cleared your plate. (You also had to drink a small bottle of warm milk at break, yuk!)

Remove the outer leaves and cut off the stalk. It should not be removed entirely, otherwise all the leaves will fall off. Cut a cross in to the base and then wash in cold water. Boil in water with a pinch of salt for 10 minutes.

Cabbage

Remove the rough outer leaves and the centre stalk. You can either shred or quarter the leaves. To cook the shredded cabbage place in boiling water for about 5 minutes. If the leaves are bigger they will need about 10 minutes.

Carrots

Top and tail the carrots and then either using a scraper or a knife remove the outer surface. Before cooking they can be quartered or sliced. Baby carrots can be cooked whole. Boil in salted water for 15 to 20 minutes. Carrots can be eaten raw in salads etc. They can also be roasted in oil when cooking a roast dinner.

Cauliflower
Wash in cold water and then divide into flowerets. Boil in salted water until tender - this should take about 10 minutes depending on the size of the flowerets. Cauliflower can also be eaten raw and used as a crudité.

Courgettes
Having been force-fed these for years I have almost come to like them. First of all give them a wash, then top and tail them. Slice thinly and fry in butter or oil for about 10 minutes. Alternatively boil for approximately 5 minutes.

Leeks
Remove the dark green section of the stalk and the and wash. They can either be sliced into rings, quartered or even left whole. To cook either boil for 10 to 15 minutes or fry in oil or butter for about 10 minutes.

Mange-tout
If you haven't seen these before, they look like pea pods that have been squashed by a lorry. But they taste delicious and are arguably worth the extortionate amount you will be charged for them.

To prepare your mange-tout, wash, top and tail. If boiling, they need only 3 or 4 minutes because they maintain their flavour better when still crisp. They can also be fried gently in butter for a few minutes until they soften slightly. They make a colourful addition to stir fries.

Mushrooms

The many types of mushroom available range from the standard button variety to the more exotic oyster or shittaki. Some mushrooms can be eaten raw but always wash them first. Wipe them with a damp cloth. Either remove or trim the stalk and then slice or leave whole. The mushrooms can be fried or grilled. To fry, melt a little oil or butter in a frying pan and cook for about 3 to 4 minutes, depending on size. To grill, put under a hot grill with a light covering of butter. Mushrooms can be a great addition to many sauces.

Onions

The best way to stop your eyes watering when chopping onions is to get someone else to do it. Top and tail the onion first, then peel off the outer layer. It can be chopped vertically or sliced into rings. Onions are normally fried in oil for about 5 minutes. They can be boiled in salted water for about 10 minutes. When frying onions take care that you don't burn them as this can taint a whole meal even if only a few of the onions are burnt.

Parsnips

Top and tail, then peel and chop into largish pieces or thick slices. They can be boiled, fried or roasted.

Place in boiling water with a pinch of salt for about 20 minutes or until they are tender. If they are to be fried they need to be cut into thin slices or chips, otherwise they will not cook all the way through. Perhaps the nicest way of cooking parsnips is to bake them. Place the parsnips in an ovenproof dish with a couple of tablespoons of oil, and bake in a hot oven for about 40 minutes. They can be basted as if they were roast potatoes.

Peas

If you have fresh peas, ie still in the pod, shell them and wash in cold water. To cook the peas, place them in boiling water for about 10 minutes.

Peppers

Available in red, green, yellow and orange. They all have different flavours - the lighter in colour they are the sweeter they are, so the yellow ones are the sweetest and the green ones the most bitter.

Top and tail, then remove all the core and seeds. Slice into rings then halve and fry in a little oil for 5 minutes or so.
They can also be eaten raw and are particularly tasty in salads. Try one of the stuffed pepper recipes that are in this book as a third alternative.

Potatoes

Just as the Italians have their pasta, we seem to be mad about potatoes. We serve them in various guises, be it chips, crisps, roasted, boiled or mashed.

There are two basic types of potato: 'new' and 'old'. Both are now available all year round, although new potatoes are cheaper in the summer. Allow 1 or 2 potatoes per person, depending on your appetite and the size of the potato.

All potatoes need to be peeled or scrubbed before cooking, unless you are preparing jacket potatoes.

Boiled:

After peeling or scrubbing the potato, cut into halves or quarters, depending on its size, then place in salted boiling water for 15 to 20 minutes or until they are tender all the way through.

Mashed:

If you want mashed potato make sure they are well cooked: you should be able to pass a knife through them easily. If they are not well cooked you find that the mashed potatoes have lumps in, however hard you try to remove them. Drain the potatoes, add a nob of butter and a drop of milk, then using a potato masher squash until they are nice and creamy, adding more milk and black pepper if required.

Roast Potatoes

There are a number of ways to produce roast potatoes. Obviously having a potato and an oven is a good starting point. Peel the potatoes, then halve or quarter them depending on their size. Parboil for 5 minutes in salted boiling water, then drain. Drain the potatoes in a colander and shake so that the surface of the potatoes are slightly flaky (this produces crisp edges). Place the semi-cooked potatoes in a baking tray with some oil or lard and place in the oven on Gas Mark 6 (425 Deg F, 220 Deg C) near the top of the oven if possible. Baste the potatoes with the oil a couple times while they are cooking. Roast the potatoes until they are golden and verging on crispiness, this should take between 60 and 90 minutes.

Chips

These are a British institution, and they should of course be served with fish and wrapped in an old newspaper with lashings of vinegar and salt. If that description hasn't quelled your craving for chips then here is how to make your own. Peel some old potatoes and cut into chip shapes. If you are feeling sophisticated slice them thinner into French fries. The next stage is potentially dangerous so take care. The chips need to be covered (at least partially) in oil to cook, so a large amount of oil is needed.

Heat the oil in a large frying pan. To test if the oil is hot enough drop one chip in - if the oil bubbles loudly all around the chip it is up to temperature. Carefully add the chips, taking care not to throw them in the pan, otherwise hot oil will be splashed. Fry the chips until they are crisp, making sure that the oil does not get too hot. Remember to turn the heat off as soon as you have finished frying.

Pumpkin

If you have a whole pumpkin, cut it into 4 then remove all the seeds and pulp from the inside. Remove the skin and cut into chunks. To boil, place in salted boiling water for about 30 minutes. After the pumpkin has been boiled it can be fried in butter for 5 minutes.

Spinach
When buying spinach, buy more than you would if it was cabbage, for spinach will shrink considerably during cooking. Discard any yellowed leaves, then place in a small amount of boiling water for about 10 minutes. Grated nutmeg and spinach taste good together.

Swede
Peel and chop into chunks, then wash in cold water. Cook in salted boiling water for 20 to 25 minutes or until tender. Can be mashed with a nob of butter and black pepper.

Sweetcorn
Remove the husks and the ends, then place in boiling water for 10 minutes. Drain, then serve with butter and fresh black pepper.

Tomato
Fresh tomatoes can be fried in butter, grilled or baked. To remove the skin of a tomato, which should be done when making sauces, place in boiling water for about a minute. Remove from the hot water and cool them in cold water. The skins should now come away with ease.

Turnip
Peel and cut into chunks, then place in boiling water for 20 to 25 minutes or until tender.

Spices, Herbs, Seasonings
And Flavourings

Cooking without herbs and spices is like looking at the world in black and white. There is something missing, a certain blandness. Given moderate use, spices, herbs and seasonings can transform a plain tasting meal into something special. Spices from around the world are available in most supermarkets, so it is possible to recreate authentic cuisine from as far afield as Thailand to Torquay. Just remember the amounts used have to be carefully controlled, the idea being to enhance the flavour of the food, not to annihilate your taste buds. Many spices are available in different strengths such as chilli and curry powder, and there is sometimes a difference between brands, so go on the side of caution.

When the recipes say salt and pepper it generally means a pinch of each, but it is up to the individual to season according to taste. One of the most essential items in a kitchen is a pepper mill. Freshly ground pepper tastes so much better than the pre-ground stuff. If you wish to cut down on your salt intake use a salt substitute, there are several on the market.

If you have a garden why not grow your own herbs? Mint, rosemary, sage, thyme and sorrel all flourish in our climate. Basil does not fair so well lacking the intense flavour that is found from the imported product.

Garlic

Whenever the word garlic is mentioned it provokes the same old comments about smelly breath and how useful it is for keeping vampires away. What they should be talking about is how it is one of the most vital ingredients in cooking. Garlic is related to the onion. Although normally associated with France it is believed that it originated from Asia, where it is still used in abundance. As well as the white skinned garlic it can also be found with a pink or even light purple covering. The only difference is that they seem to taste a little milder than the white.

When choosing garlic look for firm undamaged bulbs. Should you see any sign of green shoots appearing from the top of the bulb, don't buy it. Garlic that is past its best will dry out and be unusable. Although buying large quantities of garlic may look attractive when it is hanging in your kitchen, unless you use it on a regular basis it is likely to go off.

Garlic should be stored in a dry place, and although hanging it in the kitchen may provide the kitchen with bit of rustic charm it is not the ideal place, as the temperature fluctuates, and there is a high degree of moisture. Special terracotta garlic pots are good if you are only keeping small quantities.

When using garlic it is a matter of preference as to how much is used, depending on the required flavour of the dish. It is not only the amount of garlic that is used that will effect how strong the taste of garlic will be, the method of preparation and cooking of the garlic will also contribute.

Garlic can be used to give a subtle addition to a salad by rubbing the inside of a salad bowl with a clove of garlic. When garlic is uncooked and used raw it is in its most powerful state; cooking garlic reduces its potency. Garlic can be sliced, chopped, or crushed according to the flavour required. Slicing gives the most mild effect, then chopping and finally crushing. Devices such as garlic presses are useful but I find that they are a bind to clean thoroughly.

Stocks

Although it is easy to be tempted into using a stock cube, you'd be surprised at the improvement in a recipe that uses fresh stock, especially in soups and casseroles. There are three basic stocks which are outlined below, but many others can be made for specialist dishes. Fresh stocks should only be kept in the fridge for a maximum of three days but they are ideal for freezing. They can also be frozen in ice cube trays, so that the amount can be carefully controlled and used as and when required.

Beef Stock

Ingredients

2 lb (1kg) beef bones
1 tbs of oil
Water
2 carrots, peeled and chopped
1 onion, peeled and quartered
6 black peppercorns
1 bouquet garni
Salt

Heat the oil in a large stock pan, then fry the onions and carrots for five minutes. After frying the vegetables, add the bones, peppercorns, bouquet garni and cover with cold water. Bring the pan to the boil slowly, removing any scum that will inevitably rise to the surface. A slotted spoon is useful for removing the scum.

After the stock has been brought to the boil it must be simmered for at least three hours, the longer it is simmered the more intense the flavour of the stock. Whilst the stock is simmering some fat will rise to the surface. This should be removed with a fat skimmer or kitchen towel. If the water level gets low add a little more.

After three or four hours remove the pan from the cooker and strain. When strained, leave to cool and then remove any remaining fat.

Fish Stock

If you are squeamish, then this is one recipe that perhaps you will want to avoid.

Ingredients

2 lb (1kg) of fish trimmings, including bones, tails, head
1 onion, peeled and quartered
1 stick of celery, chopped
1 carrot, peeled and chopped
6 peppercorns

Put all the ingredients in a large saucepan and cover with water, roughly about two pints (1 litre). Bring to the boil, removing any scum that rises to the surface. Simmer for 25 minutes then strain. It is important that the stock is not simmered for any longer than 25 minutes as the fish bones can give off a bitter taste.

Strain the stock through a fine sieve. To increase the flavour of the stock, after it has been strained it can be returned to the pan and reduced.

Court Bouillon

Court bouillon is traditionally used for poaching fish, giving a subtlety that is well worth the effort.

Ingredients

2 pints (1 litre) water
1 carrot peeled and chopped
1 stick celery, chopped
1 onion, peeled and sliced
8 peppercorns
1 bay leaf
1/4 pint (150ml) vinegar
Salt

Place all the ingredients in a large saucepan, bring to the boil then simmer for about 20 minutes. Leave to cool before using.

Chicken Stock

Chicken stock is traditionally used for poaching salmon. It is left in a dish on the river bank, and the salmon (who love the taste of chicken) jump out of the water to taste it. This is when you catch them in your net. Probably.

Ingredients

1 whole chicken carcass
1 tbs of oil
1 onion, peeled and quartered
2 carrots, peeled and chopped
3 peppercorns
1 bouquet garni
Salt

Prepare the chicken stock using the same method as for the beef stock.

Savoury Sauces

There is the potential for an almost unlimited number of sauces, and they can be used to brighten up a plain tasting dish or act as a harmonious accompaniment. The many sauces are based on a small number of elementary ingredients and once the fundamentals are mastered the possibilities are infinite. Not all sauces are simple, in fact some are downright difficult, so patience is imperative and a little confidence is helpful. The secret to a successful sauce is not to rush it and don't take any short cuts.

White Sauce

This is one of the most used sauces to which other ingredients can be added.

Ingredients

3/4 oz (20g) flour
1/2 pint (300ml) milk
1 oz (25g) butter
Salt
Pepper

Melt the butter in a small saucepan, but don't let it brown. Then stir in the flour and cook gently for a couple of minutes. The combination of butter and flour is called a Roux, and it is also the name of the method of preparation.

Remove the Roux from the heat and add a little of the milk. It has to be added gradually otherwise it will end up being lumpy. Stir the milk in until a smooth consistency is achieved, then progressively add the rest of the milk. When all the milk has been added return the pan to the heat and bring to the boil. Simmer for 3 to 5 minutes or until the sauce has thickened, stirring the sauce as it cooks. Season as required.

Cheese Sauce

This sauce is particularly saucy. It's sparkly, popular and fun to talk to, and is used in many of the recipes in this book, such as lasagna or cauliflower cheese.

Ingredients

1/2 pint (300ml) of milk
2 oz (50g) of grated cheese
3/4 oz (20g) of butter
3/4 oz (20g) of plain flour
Salt
Pepper

Repeat the method as for the white sauce, except after the sauce has been brought to the boil add the cheese. Stir in the cheese, then simmer until it has completely melted.

Parsley Sauce

Not as saucy as cheese sauce, but slightly more saucy than a bikini, parsley sauce is normally served with fish, but can be served with almost anything.

Ingredients

1/2 pint (300ml) milk
3/4 oz (20g) of plain flour
3/4 oz (20g) of butter
4 tbs of chopped fresh parsley
Salt
Pepper

As White Sauce. The parsley is added just before serving.

Mayonnaise

Once you have made your own mayonnaise you will be loathed to return to the prefabricated variety: there is no comparison. There is even better news to come - once you have mastered making mayonnaise you can go on to make aïoli. This Provençal speciality is totally Moorish, the only dilemma is that its main flavouring is garlic!

Ingredients

2 egg yolks
2 tsp of white wine vinegar
1/2 pint (300ml) of olive oil
Squirt of lemon juice
1 tsp of smooth French mustard
Salt
Pepper

Put the egg yolks into a mixing bowl with the mustard and mix together. Then slowly begin to add the olive oil. The main problem with making mayonnaise is that it can curdle if the oil is added too quickly. Mayonnaise is time consuming to make, but it is essential to take care. A fine drizzle of oil is needed and has to be controlled with total precision; hold the bottle of oil at the bottom in the palm of your hand, this gives more control. Using a balloon whisk, beat the yolks and the oil together, you will notice that the colour is quite yellow in comparison with the bought variety, but this is the way it should be. Keep whisking the mayonnaise until all the oil is added, then add the vinegar, lemon juice, salt, pepper and mix. Taste and adjust the flavourings to suit.

This is making mayonnaise the hard way, and if you are making larger quantities you will be quite exhausted by the time you have finished. There is an alternative. Mayonnaise can be produced in a food processor, but again fine control is required and the result is not as good. Put all the ingredients, bar the oil, in the processor and switch on, then add the oil slowly.

Aïoli

This is one Provençal recipe that lacks the characteristic vibrant colours normally associated with its cuisine. What it might lack in colour it makes up for in flavour - this recipe is a knockout. It is rarely served in this country, possibly as a result of its high garlic content. You are missing out if you don't try this favourite of our Gaelic chums. Aïoli should ideally be served with freshly cooked vegetables such as courgettes, French beans, hard-boiled eggs and raw tomatoes. Serve on a large platter dish.

Ingredients

6 cloves of garlic
2 egg yolks
Juice of 1 lemon
1/2 pint (300ml) of olive oil
Salt
Pepper

Using a pestle and mortar crush the garlic with pinch of salt into a fine paste. If you don't have a pestle and mortar improvise using a small bowl and the back of a spoon. Transfer the garlic into a mixing bowl then add the egg yolks. The next stage is the same as when making mayonnaise; the oil must be added very slowly and be stirred constantly. When all the oil is added, season and add then lemon juice.

Tapenade

If you spend any time in Provence you are bound to come across certain dishes for which the region is celebrated and Tapenade is one of them. It is a paste that is named after the word Tapeno, which is French for capers. Should you ever be on holiday in the South of France and you wish to escape from the 'high life', take a trip down the coast to Cassis, which is close to Marseilles. Cassis is a small fishing port that remains unspoilt and oozes with charm. At the harbourside there is a terrace of restaurants in the harbour that serve wonderful fresh fish. Alternatively sit in one of the cafes, sip a glass of Pastis or Bandol Rose and nibble on a few olives or try some tapenade spread on toasted bread.

Serves 4

Ingredients

12 black olives, stoned
6 anchovy fillets
2 oz (50g) tinned tuna
3 tbs capers
1 clove garlic, peeled and crushed
3 tbs olive oil
1 tbs cognac

Put the olives, anchovies, capers, garlic and tuna in a food processor and blend to a paste. Then add the olive oil and cognac and mix well. The amount of olive oil used is only a guide-line, it depends on the required consistency as to how much is used.

Pesto

This recipe uses insane quantities of fresh basil, but the aroma is intoxicating. Pesto is traditionally served with pasta, but it can be spread on toast. It can be made in larger quantities and kept in a screw top jar in the fridge.

Serves 4

Ingredients

2 cloves of garlic, peeled and crushed
2 oz (50g) of pine nuts
2 cups of fresh basil leaves
3 tbs of finely grated fresh Parmesan
1/4 pint (150ml) olive oil
Salt

Put the basil leaves, pine nuts and the garlic in a blender and grind for a few seconds. Then add the cheese, oil and salt and mix well. If you are a stickler for authenticity, then you should prepare the pesto in a mortar, but a blender is far quicker.

Cranberry Sauce

Christmas, Humbug! I must confess to not being the biggest fan of Christmas. Too much kitsch, relatives, silly paper hats, noise and commotion. Then there's the shopping. There are, I suppose, a few minor compensations; the inevitable repeats of Star Wars and Chitty Chitty Bang Bang to keep all amused, and an excuse to eat copious amounts of food, accompanied by attempts to drink the country dry. At the end of the festivities you are normally left fat, broke and with a hangover that will probably stay until the Christmas carols start playing in the shops reminding us that there are only 200 shopping days until next Yuletide.

Ingredients

8 oz (225g) fresh cranberries
1/2 pint (300ml) water
4 oz (100g) sugar

Boil the water in a large saucepan then add the cranberries. Cook for about 15 minutes or until they are tender. Stir in the sugar and heat through until the sugar has dissolved. If a thinner sauce is required add a little more water.

Barbecue Sauce

I tend to make barbecue sauces out of whatever is to hand. A little of this and that can provide some interesting results. Just remember to taste the sauce before you cover your meat or vegetables in it, as you could have concocted something awful.

Ingredients

4 tbs olive oil
1 tbs honey
2 tbs tomato purée
1 garlic clove, peeled and crushed
1 tsp Tabasco
1 tsp Worcester sauce
2 tbs wine vinegar
2 tsp corn flour

Heat the oil in a small saucepan, then add the other ingredients stirring constantly. Make sure that all the ingredients are thoroughly mixed. Remove from the heat and cool. If you want to be a little more adventurous try adding other ingredients such as chutney, mustard, herbs or soy sauce.

Bread Sauce

No self-respecting turkey would be seen dead without the traditional accompaniments of bacon rolls, fresh cranberry sauce and of course bread sauce.

Ingredients

4 oz (100g) fresh white breadcrumbs
1 oz (25g) butter
3/4 pint (400ml) milk
1 onion, peeled
4 cloves
4 peppercorns
Pinch of nutmeg
1 bay leaf
Salt
Pepper

Cut the onion in two and press the cloves into the onion. Place the onion in a saucepan with the milk, bay leaf, nutmeg and peppercorns. Bring to the boil then remove from the heat and leave to infuse for 15 minutes. Strain into a bowl then pour over the breadcrumbs. Mix in the butter then return to the pan and heat until the sauce thickens.

Mint Sauce

Ingredient
Cup of fresh mint
2 tbs vinegar
2 tbs caster sugar
2 tbs hot water

Wash the mint then remove the leaves. Finely chop the leaves and place in a bowl with the sugar. Pour on the hot water and stir. Leave for 5 minutes or until the sugar has dissolved. Add the vinegar and leave to infuse for at least 2 hours.

Apple Sauce

The perfect accompaniment to roast pork.

Ingredients

1 lb (500g) cooking apples, peeled, cored, sliced
3 tbs of water
Juice of half a lemon
1/2 oz (15g) butter
2 tsp of sugar

Put the apples in a saucepan with the lemon juice, water, sugar and butter and simmer gently until the apples are soft. Take care not to burn the apples. If you want a smooth sauce put the mixture in a blender for a minute. If the sauce is too bitter add a little more sugar. To make the sauce a little special add a tablespoon of calvados.

Dressings

The use of dressings can add life to even the most miserable salad. Fresh peppers dunked in a little olive oil would constitute a dressing. By making your own dressings you can fine-tune them according to your own personal tastes. It should be remembered that a dressing should not swamp a salad. The salad should be coated not bathed. It is possible to buy ready prepared dressings but they rarely match those that are home-made.

French Dressing

Most people are familiar with French Dressing, also commonly referred to by the French name vinaigrette.

There are many variations of French dressing, and most people have there own favourite combinations. Oil and vinegar are the primary ingredients to which herbs or flavourings can be added. Olive oil is a must for an authentic tasting dressing, vegetable oil although much cheaper will not taste the same, and use a wine vinegar not malt. As with most recipes, even ones that only contain two ingredients, there are disagreements as to the correct proportions of oil and vinegar. This is yet another one of those daft arguments, the proportions should be based upon personal preference. In theory the average is 4 parts oil to 1 part vinegar. I'm not advocating this, you might prefer a less acidic flavour and use 6 parts oil, and so on.

Ingredients

4 tbs olive oil
1 tbs white wine vinegar
Salt
Pepper

What could be easier? Put the oil, vinegar, salt and pepper in a small screw top jar and shake until the two liquids have combined. After a while the oil and vinegar will separate again.

If you want a dressing out of the ordinary try adding a little mustard or fresh herbs such as basil, mint, parsley or chives. An alternative to using vinegar is to use lemon juice.

Garlic Dressing

Make as above, but add half a finely crushed clove of garlic.

Yoghurt Dressing

Ingredients

1/4 pint (150ml) of plain yoghurt
1 tbs of lemon juice
Salt
Pepper

Mix the yoghurt and lemon juice together, season according to taste.

Dips And Savoury Butters

Hummus

This is a dip of Middle Eastern origin and is easy to make. Although Hummus is available in tins, it is cheaper to make your own. Having said that, I find it easier to use canned chick peas instead of soaking dried ones for hours. Serve with pitta bread.

Note that a blender is needed for this recipe.

Ingredients

1 can of chick peas
2 cloves of garlic, peeled and finely chopped
1 tbs of tahini
Juice of one lemon
2 tbs of olive oil
1/2 tsp of ground cumin
Paprika

Put all the ingredients in a blender and let them have it! Switch off when a smooth consistency has been achieved. Then put in a dish and chill for an hour or two. Before serving dust with paprika.

Cucumber Raita

A traditional Indian dish that is served as an accompaniment to curry. If the roof of your mouth is feeling like a furnace, this might help.

Serves 2 to 4

Ingredients

1/2 cucumber, peeled and chopped into pieces
A small pot of natural yoghurt
1 tbs of olive oil
1 tbs of freshly chopped mint
Pepper
Salt

Mix the cucumber, yoghurt and mint together in a bowl, pour the oil on top, and season.

Guacamole

Serves 3 to 4

Ingredients

2 ripe avocados
3 tbs lemon juice
1 tbs olive oil
1 clove of garlic, peeled and crushed
Pinch of chilli powder
Salt
Pepper

Peel the avocados and remove the stones. Mash the flesh with a fork and add the other ingredients. Season to taste and serve with tortilla chips, raw vegetables or on toast.

Savoury Butters

Butter can be combined with other ingredients, such as herbs, garlic or mustard, and can be used to accompany a variety of meat or fish dishes or vegetables.

After preparing the butters they can be made into cylinder shapes, put into foil and then either frozen or chilled depending on when they are going to be used. When they are chilled they can be cut into slices.

Mustard Butter

This is the perfect accompaniment to grilled fish or steak.

4 oz (100g) butter
1 tbs French mustard
Salt
Pepper

Beat the ingredients up until they confess to something they didn't do, or until they are completely blended.

Anchovy Butter

4 oz (100g) butter
2 anchovy fillets
1 tsp anchovy essence

Apply unneccesary violence to the ingredients. Show them who's boss in the kitchen, and don't stop until they are completely blended.

Lemon Butter

4 oz (100g) butter
3 tsp lemon juice

As above, beat the ingredients together, be a man, don't take any nonsense from them.

Garlic Butter

Not only is this the crucial ingredient for 'garlic bread', it can be used with vegetables or meats.

4 oz (100g) butter
2 cloves of garlic, peeled and crushed
Salt
Pepper

Beat the ingredients together until they are completely submissive, demoralised and blended.

Starters

If you are going all out to impress then a pair of clean socks, an ironed shirt and a shave are a step in the right direction. Don't stop there, however. Should you want to create a special meal, make the effort to produce a starter.

Many of these recipes do not have to be served as a starter, the amounts can be increased so they can be served as a main meal.

Deep Fried Camembert

If you are having a barbeque, why not wrap a whole Camembert in foil and place it in the embers of the fire?

Serves 2

Ingredients

Vegetable oil
1 Camembert cheese
Dried white breadcrumbs
1 egg, beaten

Cut the Camembert into four then dip in the egg, followed by a roll in the breadcrumbs, making sure they are evenly coated. Put on a plate and place in the fridge for 30 minutes.

Heat the oil in deep fryer until it begins to smoke. Test the temperature by dropping a breadcrumb into the oil, it should sizzle as soon as it hits the surface. When the oil is at the correct temperature fry the Camembert until golden. Drain and then serve with redcurrant sauce.

Smoked Salmon Salad

See the recipe for making chicken stock for instructions on how to catch salmon the easy way (other than by casting your line in the supermaket fish section).

Serves 4

Ingredients

Mixed salad
4 oz (100g) smoked salmon
Lemon
Salt
Pepper
Olive oil

Arrange the salad on four small plates, so that the plate is covered with salad. Cut the salmon into small pieces then place on the salad. Drizzle lightly with olive oil then season. Serve with lemon wedges.

Moules Marinières

Moules make an excellent starter and they are cheap to buy, yet look impressive. So do mussels.

Serves 4

Ingredients

4lb (2kg) mussels
2 cloves garlic, peeled and finely chopped
4 shallots, peeled and finely chopped
2 tbs of chopped parsley
1 oz (25g) butter
1 pint (600ml) of white wine
1 bouquet garni
Salt
Pepper

Scrub the mussels and remove the beards that are usually attached to them. If there are any mussels that are already open or cracked discard them. Put the shallots, wine, garlic and parsley into a large saucepan and simmer for 5 minutes. Add the mussels and the bouquet garni, turn up the heat and cook for about 5 minutes. Then add the butter and cook for another 10 minutes. Whilst the mussels are cooking shake the pan a couple of times, this helps the mussels to open and ensures they are cooked evenly.

When cooked, remove the bouquet garni and any mussels that have not opened. Season and then serve with the juice. If a slightly stronger tasting sauce is required, reduce the sauce by boiling it rapidly for a few minutes. The mussels should be served immediately with a little chopped parsley on top.

Grilled Grapefruit

This is a very quick and tasty way of serving grapefruit. It does not have to be confined to a starter, but can be served as a snack for lunch or part of a late supper. Or an early supper. Or an early breakfast. Or at about 4.20pm.

Serves 2

Ingredients

1 grapefruit
2 tsp of soft brown sugar
1 tsp of butter
1/2 tsp of cinnamon

Cut the grapefruit in half and remove the pips. Loosen the segments using a grapefruit knife. Put a teaspoon of brown sugar on each half with the butter and a light sprinkling of cinnamon. Place under a hot grill for five minutes.

Garlic Bread

If the Roman Empire was a dinner party, its massive stone palaces were the garlic bread. No wonder the Empire collapsed.

Serves 4

Ingredients

French stick
4 oz (100g) of butter
2 cloves of garlic
Tin foil

Put the butter in a small mixing bowl. Finely chop the garlic and add to the butter, blending it in with a fork. Slice the French stick at 2 inch intervals, without actually severing it, and spread some of the butter on both sides of each slit. Then close up the gaps and wrap the loaf in foil. Place in the oven and cook for 15 to 20 minutes at Gas Mark 5 (400 Deg F, 200 Deg C).

Mini Sausages With Honey And Rosemary

In cooking it is often the most simple dishes that can be the most rewarding, and this is one such dish. Delicious.

Serves 4

Ingredients

Pack of mini sausages
Handful of fresh rosemary
3 tbs of runny honey

Arrange the sausages in a baking dish, prick with a fork, spoon on the honey, then place the rosemary on top. I find that slightly crushing the rosemary gives a stronger taste to the sausages. Bake in the oven on Gas Mark 6 (425 Deg F, 220 Deg C) for about 40 minutes, turning occasionally so they brown evenly. If you are in a hurry stick the sausages under the grill.

Mushrooms With Garlic Butter

Mushrooms like to be kept in the dark, so don't tell them any secrets.

Serves 4

Ingredients

4 oz (100g) of mushrooms
3 oz (100g) of butter
2 cloves of garlic, peeled and finely chopped

Remove the stalk of the mushrooms then wash. Mix the butter and the garlic together with a fork and then spread on top of the mushrooms. Bake in the oven for 15 minutes on Gas Mark 5 (400 Deg F, 200 Deg C).

Goat's Cheese Salad

Even if you are into strong cheese, a ripe goat's cheese can bring tears to your eyes. There are many ways of serving goat's cheese, apart from the obvious bread accompaniment. It is sometimes served with fresh figs, or in a salad.

Serves 4

Ingredients

4 small goat's cheeses
Mixed salad
Olive oil
Salt
Pepper

Arrange the salad on four small plates. Heat two tablespoons of olive oil in a small frying pan and then add the cheese. Lightly fry the cheese until it gets close to melting. Use a pan slice to remove the cheese from the pan and then place on top of the salad. Any oil that remains in the pan can be poured over the salad. Finally season.

Soups

The recipes for soup are legendary. There are thick, thin, clear, hot, cold ones, and it is possible to produce soup from almost any natural ingredients. A blender is essential if you want a smooth soup. Soups are ideal for freezing so why not make double the quantity and freeze what you don't use?

Carrot And Ginger Soup

Sometimes known as Jasper and Rogers Soup, though not very often. This is my favourite of all soups, the ginger gives it a delicious flavour that never fails to impress. Use fresh ginger, but remember to take it out before serving.

Serves 4

Ingredients

1 lb (500g) carrots, peeled and chopped
1 potato, peeled
1 piece of fresh root ginger
2 pints (1 litre) water
4 tbs single cream (optional)
Salt
Pepper

Place the carrots, potato and ginger in a pan and cover with the water. Bring to the boil and then simmer for 20 minutes. Remove from the heat and take out the ginger. Transfer the ingredients into a blender and blend until a smooth consistency is achieved. Season according to taste and stir in the cream if desired.

Tomato Soup

Still one of the most popular soups. Why not try spicing it up by adding a few pinches of chilli powder? Great for a cold winter's night or as something to eat when you feel slightly hungry.

Serves 4

Ingredients

1 lb (500g) of tomatoes
1 onion, peeled and finely chopped
1 clove of garlic, peeled and chopped
Bouquet garni
1 pint (600ml) of water
1/2 pint (300ml) of milk
1 tbs of oil
Salt
Pepper

Boil some water in a saucepan, then place the tomatoes in it. Remove the pan from the heat and leave for about 5 minutes. This is the best way of skinning a tomato. After this, remove the tomatoes from the water and peel off the skins. Chop into small pieces.

Fry the tomatoes and garlic and onions gently in the oil for about 15 minutes until they go mushy. Add the water and bouquet garni, then simmer for 1 hour. If you don't want bits in your soup, sieve the mixture. Otherwise, just add the milk to the tomato mixture and stir. Season. Simmer for about 3 minutes, then serve.

French Onion Soup

The French are passionate about their soups and most regions have their own speciality soup which reflects the area, the climate and produce. With this recipe there are no firm rules and numerous variations on the same theme occur. This is one soup that benefits from using home-made beefstock.

Serves 4

Ingredients

2 large onions, peeled and thinly sliced
2 pints (1 litre) of beef stock
2 tsp flour
1 tbs oil
4 slices French Bread
2 oz (50g) Gruyère cheese, grated
Salt
Pepper

Heat the oil in a saucepan, then fry the onions slowly for 15 minutes, until they end up a golden colour. Stir in the flour and cook for about 5 minutes, stirring the onions constantly. Add the beef stock and bring to the boil. Season and simmer for 25 minutes. 10 minutes before it is cooked preheat the grill. Divide the cheese onto the slices of bread. When the soup is ready pour it into a serving dish, (to be authentic you should have an earthenware tureen), place the slices of bread on top of the soup and place under the grill until the cheese melts. Serve immediately.

Vegetable Soup

At the end of the summer there is usually an abundance of fresh vegetables available from local nurseries. I buy vast quantities of tomatoes and make up batches of tomato sauce and soup that can be frozen and used when needed during the winter. There are no limits as to what vegetables you can use. This is just a guide-line.

Serves 4

Ingredients

2 tbs of oil
1 onion, peeled and chopped
1 leek, thinly sliced
2 cabbage leaves, shredded or finely chopped
1 courgette, finely chopped
1 carrot, scraped and sliced
1 tsp mixed herbs
1 bay leaf
2 pints (1 litre) of vegetable stock
Salt
Pepper

Heat the oil in a large saucepan, then fry the onions for about 5 minutes or until they have softened. Then add the other vegetables and fry for a further 10 minutes. Add the stock and herbs then season. Bring to the boil, then simmer for 30 minutes. Remove the bay leaf before serving. If you want a smoother texturing soup then liquidise before serving.

Curried Parsnip And Apple Soup

A liquidiser is required for this recipe.

Serves 4

Ingredients

2 tbs of oil
1 large onion, peeled and chopped
1 1/2 lb (750g) parsnips, peeled and chopped
1 apple, peeled and cored
2 tsp medium curry powder
2 pints (1 litre) of vegetable stock
Salt
Pepper

Heat the oil in a large saucepan, then fry the onions and curry powder for about 5 minutes until they have softened. Add the apple and the parsnips and fry gently for another 5 minutes. Stir in the stock and bring to the boil, then simmer for 30 minutes. Transfer the soup into a liquidiser and blend until smooth.

Serve with fresh crusty bread. If you don't like the flavour of curry then omit it.

Gazpacho

This is a thin chilled soup that is a very refreshing on a hot summer's evening. A blender is needed for this recipe. I often add a dash of Tabasco sauce, but this is optional.

Serves 4

Ingredients

8 oz (225g) ripe tomatoes, skinned
1/2 green pepper, deseeded and chopped
1/2 red pepper, deseeded and chopped
1/2 cucumber
1 pint (600ml) of tomato juice
1 onion, peeled and chopped
1 clove of garlic, peeled and chopped
2 tbs of olive oil
1 tbs tarragon vinegar
1 tbs of fresh chives
1 tbs of fresh parsley
Salt
Pepper

Chop all the vegetables into chunks and put aside a little of each for the garnish. Place all the ingredients except for the oil into a blender for 2 minutes or so. Then add the oil and seasoning, place in the fridge for at least 3 hours. A few ice cubes can be added to speed up this process, but don't add too many as it will make the soup weak. Serve with the reserved vegetables on top.

Chilled Cucumber Soup

Chilled cucumbers are fascinating vegetables. A variation on their warmer relatives, they are famous for the songs they sing to try to keep warm. Perhaps the best known of these goes, 'Please don't eat me/don't put me in your soup/I'm not a number/I'm a chilled cucumber', which was a hit in Belgium.

This is another soup that is ideal for serving during the summer months.

Serves 4

Ingredients

2 cucumbers, peeled and sliced
1 tbs of flour
1 pint of chicken stock
1/2 pint (300ml) of water
1/2 tsp of grated nutmeg
1/4 pint (150ml) of single cream
1 bay leaf
1 tbs fresh mint, chopped
Salt
Pepper

Place the cucumber into a saucepan with the water and cook until tender. Remove from the heat and then put in a blender for a minute or two until smooth. Return the cucumber to the saucepan and stir in the flour. Add the stock, seasoning and bayleaf then slowly bring to the boil. Simmer for 5 minutes then cool and strain. Once strained stir in the cream and chill in the fridge for a couple of hours. When you feel thoroughly chilled, get out of the fridge and serve the soup with a decoration of mint.

Pumpkin Soup

This recipe requires a liquidiser and a little enthusiasm for Halloween night. The soup tastes best through a witch's mask, but a goblin will suffice.

Serves 4

Ingredients

1 1/2 lb (750g) of pumpkin flesh, cut into cubes
1/2 pint (300ml) of milk
4 oz (100g) of butter
Salt
Pepper

Melt the butter in a saucepan, then fry the pumpkin until it is soft and mushy. Season, then add milk and put into a liquidiser for a minute. Put the liquid back into a saucepan and heat through, but do not boil.

Salads

Thankfully the days are long gone when a salad consisted only of a limp lettuce leaf, a tomato and a few crinkled slices of cucumber. There is an increasingly exotic selection of salad vegetables available: some supermarkets stock up to ten different varieties of lettuce alone. Salads are still more popular during the summer months when the produce is cheaper.

Tomato and Feta Salad

Serves 4

Ingredients

6 ripe tomatoes
4 oz (100g) feta cheese
10 black olives
Olive oil
Salt
Pepper

Slice the tomatoes and arrange on flat plate or platter dish. Cut the cheese into cubes or crumble into small pieces and place on top of the tomatoes. Arrange the olives on top, season, then drizzle with oil.

Alsace Salad

This is of my favourite salads. Appetites tend to be large in this region of France and being close to the border with Germany much of the cuisine is under the influence of both countries. This is not the region to visit if you are attempting to lose weight.

Serves 2

Ingredients

1 lettuce
4 rashers of bacon, cut into pieces
2 eggs
2 tomatoes, quartered
2 tbs of oil
Salt
Pepper

Heat the oil in a frying pan and fry the bacon. With this particular recipe the bacon pieces need to be verging on crispness, but don't let them burn. When they are cooked put them aside in a separate dish or bowl. Clear the pan of any debris then fry the eggs. Whilst the eggs are cooking arrange the lettuce in a serving dish with the tomatoes and the bacon. When the eggs are cooked let them cool for a minute and then place on top of the salad, then season.

Pasta Salad

It is a remarkable and little-known fact that pasta salad is named after the Greek philosopher, Pas Tasalad. During the third century BC, as the sun was going down, Pas had just finished philosophising for the day and asked his wife what was for tea. 'Salad with pasta,' she replied, rather sheepishly. 'Not again, woman,' he moaned. 'I've spent all day trying to work out if I exist, and that's the best you can come up with?' 'Sorry dear, the slave forgot to get the shopping today.' 'Forgot the shopping? What do I pay him for?' 'You don't.' 'Anyway, I'm sick of salad with pasta. I eat so much of the stuff that I wouldn't be surprised if salad with pasta got named after me.' And that's how it happened. More or less.

Serves 3 to 4

Ingredients

4 oz (100g) of pasta quills or shells
1/2 red pepper, deseeded and chopped
1/2 green pepper, deseeded and chopped
8 oz (225g) tin of tuna
3 tomatoes, sliced
3 tbs double cream
Pepper

Boil some water in a saucepan and cook the pasta for about 15 minutes or until it is tender, then drain.

Drain the oil from the tuna then mix all the ingredients together in a serving bowl and season.

Tomato and Onion Salad

A typical Provençal salad, so popular that anyone indigenous to the area would give their best goat for just a taste of it (the salad, not the goat). There is no need to carry any French Francs with you when you travel in Provence, just arm yourself with a few of these salads and you will soon find yourself with more goats than you know what to do with.

Serves 4

Ingredients

4 fresh tomatoes
1 onion
Fresh basil
Pepper
Salt
French dressing

Peel the onion and slice fairly thinly. Slice the tomatoes and arrange them on a large plate or dish. Place the onion pieces between the tomato slices. Decorate with the basil leaves, and season with plenty of freshly ground pepper. Pour the French dressing over the top.

Salad Niçoise

This salad is legendary in Provence, and is still popular in both restaurants and the home. As with many French recipes there are numerous variations on the same theme. So there is never a 'right' way!

Serves 4

Ingredients

1 lettuce
3 ripe tomatoes
1/2 small onion, thinly sliced
10 French beans cooked and cooled
3 eggs
8 oz (225g) tin of tuna
Small tin of anchovies
10 olives
French dressing

Hard boil the eggs for 8 minutes, then place in a bowl of cold water. Wash the lettuce and arrange the leaves in a large serving bowl, then add the onions and tuna (drain the oil first).

Quarter the tomatoes and place them on top of the lettuce, with the beans. Shell the eggs, cut them into quarters, and arrange them neatly on top of the tuna. Pour the dressing over the salad, and add the olives and anchovies, if required. Other ingredients that are sometimes used include radishes and peppers.

Italian Pepper Salad

There are many ways of serving peppers but this simple recipe is one of the best. (One of the worst is to jump on a large pepper with heavy boots, and to present it as a Rather Unpleasant Pancake garnished with treacle. Best avoided.)

Serves 4

Ingredients

4 large peppers (mixture of colours)
4 tbs of olive oil
Salt
Pepper

Heat the oven to the highest setting possible and then place the peppers on a tray on the top shelf. They should stay in the oven for about 20-30 minutes after the oven is up to temperature. After about 15 minutes turn the peppers over so they are evenly cooked.

Remove from the oven and put the peppers in a clean polythene bag and tie the ends together. Leave the peppers in the bag for at least 15 minutes then remove and peel off the skins. Make sure all the skin is removed, as it is burnt, it has a very strong flavour and can taint the dish.

After removing the skin, remove the stems and seeds then cut into strips. Place the peppers in a serving dish, drizzle with the oil and then season. There will normally be some residue from the peppers in the polythene bag that can be added to the dish for extra flavour.

Potato Salad

This recipe can be made with either salad cream or mayonnaise, according to taste: mayonnaise if you have taste, salad cream if you don't. Chopped fresh chives can be added if required.

Serves 4

Ingredients

5 medium sized potatoes
Mayonnaise
Salt
Pepper

If you are using new potatoes the skins can be left on, just scrub them. Place the potatoes in boiling water for 15 minutes or until a knife will pass through the centre fairly easily.

After the potatoes have cooled, cut into halves or quarters depending on the size, place in a bowl and dollop some mayonnaise on top. Mix together and season.

Chopped fresh chives can be added if you like. If you are using small new potatoes they can be left whole.

Another alternative to using mayonnaise is to place new potatoes in bowl with a couple of tablespoons of olive oil or melted butter.

Cucumber Salad

Cucumbers are very high in water content and provide little nutritional benefit, but they are refreshing to eat and have a lovely singing voice (see Chilled Cucumber Soup).

Serves 4

Ingredients

1 large cucumber
1 tbs white wine vinegar
1 tsp sugar
1 tbs olive oil
2 tbs chopped fresh chives
Salt
Pepper

Peel the cucumber and slice as thinly as possible. A mandolin is ideal for producing wafer thin slices.

Arrange the slices of cucumber on a flat plate and sprinkle generously with salt. Place another plate of a similar size on top and press down gently.

Leave in the fridge for 1 hour. Remove from the fridge and pour away the water that has been extracted. Mix the vinegar, oil and sugar together, then pour over the cucumber. Season, then sprinkle the chopped chives on top.

Coleslaw

In the year 1725, John Cole decreed that white cabbage should never be eaten with carrots or onion on a Tuesday. Cole was a village idiot, and no one obeyed his eccentric law. Thereafter, whenever cabbage, carrots and onions were eaten together on a Tuesday, reference was often made to the fact that 'Cole's Law' was being broken. The eating of Coleslaw is not currently an offence, but check with your lawyer before preparing this recipe.

Serves 4

Ingredients

8 oz (225g) of white cabbage, grated
2 carrots, scraped and grated
1 small onion, peeled and grated
5 to 6 tbs of mayonnaise
Salt
Pepper

If you have time, soak the cabbage for an hour to make it crisp. If not, it doesn't really matter. After soaking the cabbage, dry with a kitchen towel and put in a large serving bowl with the carrots and onion. Stir in the mayonnaise, and season.

There are many variations to this recipe. Additional ingredients can include chopped apple, sultanas, and nuts.

Tabouleh

Bulghur wheat is made from wheat that has been boiled, dried, then ground. As an ingredient it is widely used in countries like Morocco and Tunisia. Tabouleh is a perfect dish for serving at a buffet supper, it makes an interesting contrast to traditional salads.

Serves 4

Ingredients

6 oz (150g) of bulghur wheat
1/8 pint (60ml) of olive oil
1/2 cucumber, chopped
2 tomatoes, peeled and chopped
1 bunch of spring onions
1 bunch of parsley
8 mint leaves, chopped
Juice of one lemon
Salt
Pepper

Place the bulghur wheat in a saucepan of water. Bring to the boil, then simmer gently for 10 to 15 minutes until tender. Drain, then allow to cool.

Finely chop the parsley and the spring onions. Place the bulghur in a serving bowl, add the olive oil, parsley, mint, tomato, cucumber, spring onions, lemon juice, salt and pepper. Mix together thoroughly.

Choosing Meat

Although there are many tantalising and of course healthy vegetarian meals, the allure of meat is too strong to ignore. A fillet steak cooked to perfection with a green salad and French fries is absolutely delicious. There are exceptions, such as liver, which however it is cooked is not one of my favourites. Even less appetising is tongue.

After arriving late at a hotel one night in Tunisia with a friend we were asked whether we still wanted to eat, not wishing to turn down an offer of food my companion and I agreed. Entering the restaurant we found that it was completely empty. A rather miserable waiter who probably wanted to go home seated us by a window. There did not appear to be a choice, the first course was a watery soup which was barely edible, the next offering was a enormous plate of tongue, with no accompaniments. I would rather eat grass than tongue, and my companion was vegetarian so we were not tempted in the slightest. There seemed to be number of staff watching and waiting for us to take a mouthful but being British we weren't brave enough to complain or just leave it. Quick thinking was called for. We had noticed a couple of stray cats outside the window. I tried the window in the vain hope that whilst the waiters were not looking I could throw the tongue out to the cats who would probably enjoy it. Alas, there was a slight flaw in the plan, the window was locked. This only left Plan B, which involved wrapping the tongue up in a thin paper serviette and putting it in my blazer pocket. As the tongue was in a sauce it was not exactly pleasant, but the cats enjoyed it later.

How To Heat Your Meat

There are a number of methods for cooking meat, including grilling, frying, stewing and roasting. The decision as to which method is chosen depends on the type of meat being used, the flavour required and also health considerations.

Grilling

As the grilling process does not tenderise meat it is important to remember that only tender meat should be grilled. When grilling meat such as chops or steak, pre-heat the grill for at least 10 minutes. Grilled meats should be browned on the surface but succulent in the middle. One of the advantages of grilling is that it requires little or no fat, so is one of the healthiest methods of cooking.

Frying

There are two basic methods of frying, determined by how much fat is used - shallow or deep-fat frying.

One of the advantages of frying is that the juices and the natural fats are kept in the pan and add to the flavour of whatever is being cooked, they can also be used as a basis for sauces. When grilling meat the juices are lost in the bottom of the grill pan.

Roasting

Still a popular method and quite rightly so. A variety of meats can be roasted and they are usually basted in their own juices and fat. Less tender cuts of meat should be roasted more slowly. Joints should be basted every 20 minutes.

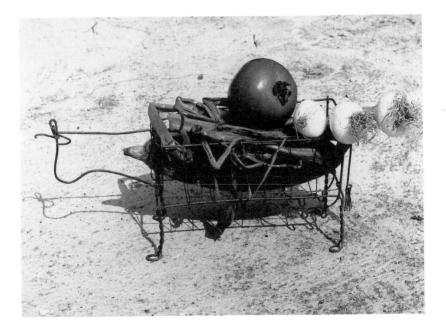

Deep frying

Special deep fryers can be purchased. Failing that use a frying pan with deep sides. Deep frying is a very quick method of cooking meat, but this method of cooking is better suited to batters or fries.

Stewing

This method is ideally suited for meat that is not particularly tender, however poultry can work well being stewed. Stewing normally involves cooking slowly in a liquid. There are two types of stew, brown and white. A brown stew is where the meat is browned before adding the other ingredients. By browning the meat the stew takes on a darker colour and the flavour will be more intense. A white stew does not involve a preliminary browning of the meat, this results in a lighter tasting and lighter coloured stew.

Choosing Meat

Beef

When choosing a piece of beef it should be a light red colour and slightly elastic, without too much gristle. Old beef appears dark in colour and the fat is often a yellow colour: avoid beef of this type.

There are many different cuts of beef, and each is suitable for different methods of cooking:

Roasting
Topside
Sirloin
Fillet
Ribs
Rump

Grilling or Frying
Sirloin
Fillet

Rump
Entrecote
Minced

Stewing
Rump
Brisket
Flank
Chuck

Pork
Pork is cheaper than beef and should be a pale pink colour, smooth on the surface and firm. In order to reduce the risk of food poisoning ensure that the pork is cooked through.

Roasting
Ribs
Loin
Leg
Bladebone

Grilling or Frying
Chops
Ribs
Loin

Lamb
Lamb should be a pinkish red colour, and the bones at the joints should be red.

Roasting
Shoulder

Leg
Best end of neck
Loin

Grilling or Frying
Loin chops or cutlets
Liver

Stewing
Loin
Leg
Breast
Liver

Chicken

Chicken is one of the cheapest of available meats as a result of factory breeding, however there has been a sacrifice in flavour in favour of price. If you want to taste how a chicken should taste, try to find a free range chicken, available from some stores. When buying chicken it should smell fresh and the flesh should be firm. Chicken is very versatile: most parts can be fried, roasted, stewed etc.

Carving Meat
There is definitely an art to carving, and it does take time to become a proficient carver. The most important thing about carving is having a sharp knife. It is very difficult to try to cut thin slices with a blunt knife. Get into the habit of sharpening the knife before use.

When cutting meat, cut across the grain, this makes it easier to chew, which is important if the meat is on the tough side. The meat should be cut with a gentle sawing action so that straight, whole slices are cut.

Usually when carving roast meat juice from the meat, forms at the bottom of the carving plate. Use these juices when making gravy. When carving a leg of lamb, it can be cut parallel to the bone.

MEAT

Spicy Sausage Casserole

This recipe is perfect for a cold winter's evening. Wash it down with a robust wine with plenty of kick. If you really want to turn up the heat add more chilli powder, or a couple of fresh chillies, or simply put another log on the fire.

Serves 4

Ingredients

1 pack of pork sausages, cut into pieces
1 onion, peeled and chopped
2 cloves of garlic, peeled and finely chopped
1 tin of tomatoes (14 oz)
2 tbs of tomato purée
1 green pepper, deseeded and chopped
Glass of red wine
2 tsp of chilli powder
1 tsp of oregano
2 tbs of oil
Pepper
Salt

Heat the oil in a largish saucepan or wok, then fry the onions, garlic and chilli powder for about 5 minutes. Add the sausages and the pepper, and cook for about 10 minutes. Add the tomato purée, wine, seasoning, tomatoes and oregano. Simmer for at least 15 minutes then serve with rice and peas. Alternatively, after cooking the rice and peas add them directly to the casserole and cook for another couple of minutes. Also tastes nice with grated cheese on top.

Pork Provençal

This dish is based on a recipe from the Hotel du Commerce in Castellane. The food and service there is almost as inspiring as the breathtaking scenery nearby. As with most Provençal food there is the usual delectable combination of garlic, onions, tomatoes and herbs.

Serves 4

Ingredients

4 pork steaks/chops
1 onion, chopped and peeled
1 clove of garlic, peeled and finely chopped
1 tin of tomatoes (14 oz)
1 red pepper, deseeded and finely chopped
2 tsp of herbes de Provence
1 finely chopped courgette
4 slices of cheddar cheese
2 tbs of oil
Salt
Pepper

Fry the onion and garlic in the oil for about 5 minutes. When these have cooked, add the tomatoes, red pepper, courgette, herbs, salt and pepper. Let the sauce simmer for 20 minutes. After 10 minutes, grill the pork on foil, turning once. When it is nearly cooked put some sauce and the slices of cheese on the pork and grill until the cheese begins to melt.

Serve with potatoes and fresh vegetables and the rest of the sauce.

Shepherd's Pie

This popular dish is supposed to use leftover beef from a Sunday roast, but minced beef is an adequate substitute for those not indulging in a roast. This recipe has many variations: I prefer to use the one that includes tomatoes, but try both and see which one you like.

Serves 3 to 4

Ingredients

1 lb (500g) of minced beef
1 onion, peeled and chopped
1 clove of garlic, peeled and finely chopped
1 tin of tomatoes (14 oz), optional
1 tbs of tomato purée
1 tsp of mixed herbs
2 tbs of oil
5 medium potatoes, peeled
Butter
Milk
Salt
Pepper

Heat the oil in a largish saucepan, add the onion and garlic, and fry for 3 to 4 minutes. Add the meat and cook for another 10 minutes, then add the other ingredients, (except potatoes, butter and milk) and simmer for 15 minutes.

While this is simmering, cook the potatoes (test them with a knife - the knife should pass through the potato easily), then mash them with a nob of butter and a drop of milk. Put the meat in an ovenproof dish and cover with the potato, then put under the grill until the potato turns a golden brown.

Pork Stir Fry

Serves 2

Ingredients

2 tbs of oil
8 oz (225g) of diced pork
1 green pepper, deseeded and chopped
1 onion, peeled and chopped
1 tsp of chilli powder
1 clove of garlic, peeled and sliced
1 tbs of soy sauce
Salt
Pepper

Heat the oil in a large frying pan or wok, then fry the onions and the garlic for about 3 to 4 minutes. Add the pepper, soy sauce and the pork. Fry until the pork is cooked the season. This should take about 10 minutes, depending on the size of the meat pieces. Serve with rice.

Moussaka

Serves 4

Ingredients

1 large aubergine, sliced
2 large potatoes, parboiled and sliced
2 onions, peeled and chopped
1 tin of tomatoes (14 oz)
1 tbs of tomato purée
1 clove of garlic, crushed and finely chopped
1 lb (500g) of minced beef or lamb
2 tbs of oil
1 oz (25g) of butter
1 oz (25g) of flour
3/4 pint (375ml) of milk
4 oz (100g) of grated cheese
Salt
Pepper

Sprinkle the aubergines generously with salt and leave for 30 minutes. Then rinse and pat dry with kitchen paper. Heat a tablespoon of oil in a frying pan and fry the aubergines until they are soft. Then place on a piece of kitchen towel to absorb the fat. Put some more oil in the frying pan if needed and fry the onions, garlic, and meat. After about 10 minutes season, and add the tomatoes and purée.

Grease a casserole dish with either butter or oil, and fill it with alternate layers of aubergine and meat, finishing with a layer of sliced potatoes.

To make the cheese sauce, melt the butter in a saucepan, add the flour, and mix together. Remove from the heat, and very gradually add the milk. Boil until the sauce thickens, then remove from the heat and add 3 oz (75g) of the cheese. Pour the cheese sauce over the top of the aubergine, and sprinkle the rest of the cheese on top.

Bake for 40 minutes on Gas Mark 5 (200 Deg C, 400 Deg F).

Sweet And Sour Pork

There are many variations to this recipe. I tend to work on the principle of using whatever is to hand. There are obviously certain base ingredients, but to obtain the sweet and sour a variety of different ingredients can be used. As with most recipes there is no such thing as a right and wrong way, there are just different ways. Many people get terribly agitated if they see someone cooking a recipe in a slightly unusual manner. This is crazy, as long as you like it and whoever you are serving it to doesn't have any objections, convention can go out the window.

Serves 4

Ingredients

2 tbs oil
1 lb (500g) pork, cubed
1 red pepper, deseeded and chopped
1 green pepper, deseeded and chopped
2 cloves of garlic, peeled chopped
1 courgette, sliced
1 onion, peeled and roughly chopped
1 tbs dark brown sugar
2 tbs of soy sauce
1 tbs of Worcester sauce
3 tbs of tomato purée
2 tbs of wine vinegar
4 tbs of water
Pinch of chilli powder
Salt
Pepper

Heat the oil in a wok or large frying pan and then gently fry the onion and garlic for 5 minutes. Add the peppers, courgettes and fry for another couple of minutes. Take care that none of the vegetables burns. Mix the other ingredients, except for the pork, together in a small bowl or jug, then add to the wok. Add the pork and fry until the meat is cooked. Serve with rice or pasta. I find that mixing cooked pasta into the sweet and sour mixture is delicious.

Jambalaya

This is perhaps one of the ultimate Cajun recipes. A friend of mine from Louisiana introduced me to this recipe a couple of years ago - she made it using sausages and chicken, although apparently back home she said they also add alligator. It sounded interesting, but they always seem to be out of alligator steaks in Sainsbury's whenever I ask, so you will have to make do with chicken etc.

The sausages that are used in Cajun cooking are different to the British banger. One of the most widely used is of the chorizo variety. If you can't find any then ordinary sausages will do. It is important to remember that in most recipes the ingredients given are guide-lines, and that a lack of one particular item should not preclude you from attempting that recipe (unless, of course, you're trying to make toast without any bread etc). But generally speaking be brave and make up your own variation or concoction.

Serves 4

Ingredients

2 tbs of oil
2 chicken breasts, cut into pieces
8 oz (225g) of sausage (chorizo if available)
8 oz (225g) of rice
1 onion, peeled and chopped
2 cloves of garlic, peeled and finely chopped
1 green pepper, deseeded and chopped into pieces
2 sticks of celery, chopped
1 tsp of Cayenne pepper
1 pint (600ml) of vegetable/chicken stock
Salt
Pepper

Heat the oil in a large saucepan or a wok. Fry the onions and garlic for about five minutes, add the sausage and chicken and fry for another 5 minutes, then add the pepper and celery. Continue frying for another couple of minutes, then season and add the Cayenne pepper. Pour the stock over the top and bring to the boil.

When the stock is boiling add the rice and cook for roughly 20 minutes or until the rice is soft when pinched. Be careful not to over-cook the rice.

Goulash

This dish traditionally uses veal, but beef is normally used due to the controversy surrounding the methods by which veal is produced.

Serves 4

Ingredients

2 tbs of oil
1 large onion, peeled and chopped
1 lb (500g) of potatoes, peeled and sliced
1 clove of garlic, peeled and finely chopped
1 lb (500g) of cubed stewing beef
1 red pepper, deseeded and chopped
1 green pepper, deseeded and chopped
1/2 tsp of caraway seeds
1 tbs of paprika
1 tsp of mixed herbs
1 beef stock cube
3/4 pint (375ml) of boiling water
4 oz (100g) of sliced mushrooms
1 tin of tomatoes (14 oz)
1/4 pint (150ml) of soured cream, optional
Salt
Pepper

Heat the oil in a casserole dish or a large saucepan, then fry the onions and garlic for a couple of minutes. Add the meat, peppers, tomatoes, mixed herbs, paprika, caraway seeds, salt and pepper, and cook for about 5 minutes.

Dissolve the stock cube in the boiling water and add to the above. Simmer for about 40 minutes, then add the potatoes and cook for another 40 minutes. After about 30 minutes add the mushrooms. If they are added any earlier they will be over-cooked and go mushy.

Before serving add the soured cream, if required.

Chilli Con Carne

If there is one recipe most men can cook then it has to be chilli. The chilli can be made as hot as required, but remember that even though you may love to sweat, your guests might prefer it a little milder. It can be served with rice, potatoes or pitta bread. Chilli tastes pretty good even when cold, and it has been known for me to dig into the leftovers for breakfast. I usually add a green or red pepper.

Serves 4

Ingredients

2 tbs of oil
3 tsp of chilli powder
1 lb (500g) of minced beef or stewing steak
1 large onion, peeled and chopped
2 cloves of garlic, peeled and finely chopped
1/4 pint (150ml) of beef stock
1 tin of tomatoes (14 oz)
1 tin of kidney beans, drained (15 oz)
1 tsp of oregano
1 tbs of tomato purée
Glass of red wine, optional
Salt
Pepper

After frying the onions, chilli powder and garlic in the oil for about 5 minutes, mix in the mince. Cook the mince for

about 10 minutes stirring constantly to stop it burning. Add the other ingredients, except the kidney beans, varying the amounts of seasoning according to taste. Bring to the boil then simmer for about 20 minutes (the longer the better). 5 minutes before serving add the kidney beans.
Serve with rice or jacket potatoes.

Toad In The Hole

A classic dish that is about as misleading as hedgehog crisps.

Serves 4

Ingredients

1 lb (500g) of sausages
1 oz (25g) of lard
4 oz (100g) of flour
1 egg
1/2 pint (300ml) of milk
A pinch of salt

Mix the flour and the salt, then make a well in the flour and break the egg into the well. Add first a little milk to give a smooth texture, then pour in the rest of the milk and beat for a minute or so. Put the sausages in a baking tin with the lard and bake for 10 minutes at Gas Mark 7 (450 Deg F, 230 Deg C). Then add the batter and cook for a further 25 minutes or until the batter has risen and is browned.

Beef Stew

This dish is not at all misleading. Just ask Stew.

Serves 4

Ingredients

1 lb (500g) of stewing steak
1 onion, peeled and roughly chopped
1 clove of garlic, peeled and finely chopped
1 1/2 oz (40g) of flour
1 pint (600ml) of beef stock
3 carrots, scraped and chopped
Bouquet garni
2 tbs of oil
Salt
Pepper

Put the oil in a casserole dish and fry the onions and garlic for 5 minutes. Cut the meat into 1 inch (2.5cm) pieces and roll them in the flour with a little salt and pepper. Fry for 5 minutes or until brown, and add to the onion. Add the rest of the flour to the pan and fry gently. Add the stock and boil until it thickens. Pour the sauce over the meat, add the bouquet garni and carrots, and bake at Gas Mark 4 (350 Deg F, 180 Deg C) for one to two hours.

Liver With Bacon

Liver: even the name to me is unappealing. The good news is that liver is good for you. The bad news is that it is only good for you if you eat it.

Serves 4

Ingredients

2 tbs of oil
1 lb (500g) of liver
1 large onion, peeled and chopped
3 rashers of whatever bacon you can lay your hands on
Flour for coating the liver
Pepper

Coat the liver in the flour. After heating the oil in a frying pan, add the onion and fry for about 5 minutes. Add the bacon and liver to the onions, season, and cook for about 10 to 15 minutes.

Cassoulet

This is yet another classic French dish that is as far removed from nouvelle cuisine as is possible. It is a hearty dish that is particularly filling, and for an authentic cassoulet it is essential that preserved goose or duck is used. Unfortunately it is expensive and difficult to obtain, but well worth the effort if you do. This dish, due to the nature of the ingredients, is not suitable for making in small quantities - think big!

Serves 12

Ingredients

2 lb (1kg) white beans
12 pieces preserved goose or duck
2 tbs lard
8 oz (225g) salt pork, cubed (save rind)
1 lb (500g) Toulouse sausage
2 cloves garlic, crushed
4 tbs bread crumbs
1 bouquet garni
6 tomatoes, skinned, chopped
1 tbs tomato purée
2 tbs chopped parsley
1 tsp thyme

Bearing in mind the large quantities of ingredients a large casserole pot is needed.

Having soaked the beans overnight in cold water, rinse and cover with fresh water, add the pork rind, bouquet garni, garlic and bring to the boil, then simmer for 90 minutes. Whilst the beans are simmering fry the sausage, pork, goose pieces in the lard until browned then add the tomatoes, purée and herbs and a few tablespoons of water.

Skim any scum that might have risen to the surface of the beans then drain, saving about a pint of the liquid. In a large casserole dish place layers of beans, tomatoes, and meat, adding a little stock with and finishing with a layer of meat. Cover with the breadcrumbs then place in the oven for 90 minutes. Gas Mark 3 (170 Deg C, 325 Deg F). If the cassoulet begins to dry out add a little more water.

Corned Beef Hash

This recipe proves that simple inexpensive ingredients combined can create a tasty meal.

Serves 4

Ingredients

2 tbs of oil
1 tin of corned beef
1 large onion, peeled and chopped
Milk
Butter
4 large potatoes
Salt
Pepper

Peel the potatoes and chop them into quarters. Place the potatoes in a saucepan of boiling water and boil for about 20 minutes or until tender. Drain them and mash with a little milk and butter.

Whilst the potatoes are cooking fry the onions in a large frying pan with the oil for about 5 minutes or until they are golden. Open the tin of beef and chop up into small pieces and add to the onion.

Heat the beef through which will take about 5 minutes and then add the mashed potato. Fry the mixture until the potato turns slightly crispy, but not burnt.

Best served with baked beans.

Courgette and Bacon Bake

Bacon and courgettes go together as well as the letters 'B' and 'C'.

Serves 4

Ingredients

2 tbs of oil
2 lb (1 kg) of courgettes, sliced
4 oz (100g) of bacon, cut into pieces
5 oz (125g) of grated cheddar cheese
4 eggs
3/4 pint (350ml) of milk
Salt
Pepper

Fry the courgettes for 4 to 5 minutes, then add the bacon and fry for another couple of minutes. Beat the eggs together with the milk, add the cheese and season. Grease a baking dish and layer the courgettes and bacon until they are used up. Pour the egg and cheese mixture over the courgettes, put the rest of the cheese on top, and bake at Gas Mark 4 (350 Deg F, 180 Deg C) for 40 minutes or until golden.

Sausages

The banger is an amazing invention: versatile, timeless, classless and sausage-shaped. After all these years it still provides a cheap, simple and cholesterolly dangerous meal. Sausages come in various types, the most popular variants containing either pork or beef but is possible to buy more exotic varieties made from venison or wild rabbit. The price will depend on their fat content - the cheapest might be almost pure tubes of fat. Handmade sausages can still be found at some local butcher shops.

Before cooking your sausages, get a fork and stab them a couple of times. This prevents splitting.

The usual methods for cooking sausages are frying or grilling. For those who want to minimise the relative unhealthiness of the sausage, grilling is the better way to choose.

To fry: heat some oil in a frying pan, and fry the sausages for 15 to 20 minutes. Turn them regularly when cooking to make sure they brown and cook evenly.

To grill: remember to prick the sausages, then grill for about 10 minutes on each side, on a medium heat.

Lamb Casserole

Serves 4

Ingredients

2 tbs of oil
4 lamb chops
1 onion, peeled and sliced
2 leeks, sliced
8 oz (225g) of carrots, scraped and chopped
4 oz (100g) of peas
1 pint (600ml) of beef/vegetable stock
Salt
Pepper

Heat the oil in a frying pan then fry the chops for a couple of minutes on each side. Then add the onion, carrots and leek, and fry for a few more minutes. Transfer into a casserole dish, season, and pour the stock over. Put a lid on the dish and place in the oven on Gas Mark 4 (350 Deg F, 180 Deg C) for about 1 hour. Add the peas about 10 minutes before serving.

Roast Dinners

A home-cooked roast dinner is still a favourite and rightly so. For those men wanting to impress, a roast is a good place to start. Choose a nice piece of meat and serve it with fresh vegetables and either new or roast potatoes.

Remember that when using the oven, it should be switched on 20 minutes before the joint is put in to heat it up to the correct temperature.

Roast Beef

Serves 2 to 20
(according to whether you have a small joint or a whole cow)

Ingredients

1 joint of beef (topside)
1/4 pint (150ml) of vegetable oil
Gravy
Salt
Pepper

Before throwing away the packaging for your joint, note how much it weighs. Allow 20 minutes cooking time per lb, plus 20 minutes on top, all at Gas Mark 7 (450 Deg F, 230 Deg C). This will cook the meat 'English style', ie with little or no blood seeping out. If you prefer it 'rare', cook for about 15 minutes less.

Put the joint in a roasting tin and pour the oil over the top and the sides. Season with the salt and pepper, and stick in the oven.

The joint must be 'basted' - that means to spoon the oil in the tin over the top of the meat to stop it from drying out. Do this two or three times.

When the meat is cooked, carve the joint and serve with fresh vegetables. Gravy can be made from the juices in the roasting tin.

Roast Pork

This must be cooked for a little longer than beef, for it is essential that pork is well cooked. Prepare in the same method as the beef but cook for 25 minutes per pound plus 25 minutes over, on the same oven setting. Baste the joint every 20 minutes. If you like garlic place pieces of garlic into the joint before cooking.

Roast Chicken

It is important not to over-cook chicken as it loses all its flavour and is harder to carve.

Place the chicken in a baking tin with 1/4 pint of oil and season with plenty of black pepper. Bake for 15 to 20 minutes per pound plus 20 minutes on Gas Mark 6 (425 Deg F, 225 Deg C).

Roast Lamb

Lamb is expensive but has a wonderful flavour that makes it worth splashing out on occasionally. Unlike pork, it can be served pink in the middle.

Prepare in the same method as the beef and cook for 20 minutes per pound and 20 minutes over on the same oven setting. Baste every 20 minutes. Place sprigs of fresh rosemary on the lamb for added flavour.

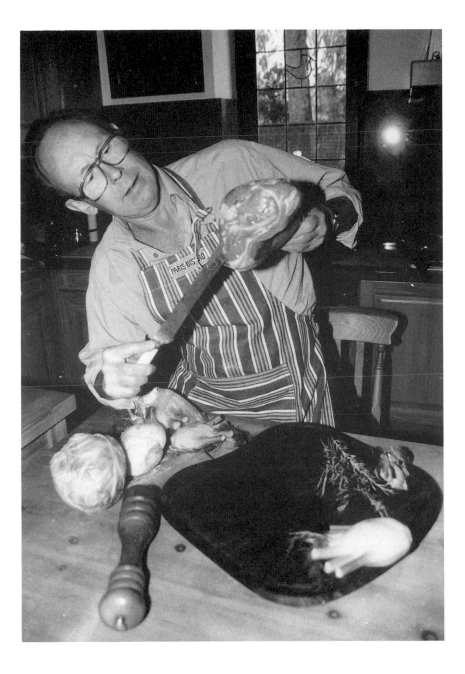

CHICKEN

Chicken Casserole

Serves 4

Ingredients

4 pieces of chicken (either breast, wings or thigh)
1/2 pint (300ml) of chicken stock
1 tbs of tomato purée
1 onion, peeled and chopped
2 tsp of flour
2 tsp of oregano or mixed herbs
Salt
Pepper

Mix the flour with a little water and then combine with the chicken stock. Add the herbs, onion, tomato purée, salt and pepper. Put the chicken in an ovenproof dish, and pour the stock over it. Cover the dish with foil and bake in the oven for 45 minutes. Serve with potatoes and vegetables.

Stuffed Chicken

If you are short of time you don't have to marinate the chicken, but you won't get the full benefit of all the flavours. If you are short of chicken you've got problems.

Serves 4

Ingredients

2 tbs of olive oil
4 chicken breasts
Juice of one lemon
2 cloves of garlic, peeled and finely chopped
2 tsp of herbes de provence
Boursin cheese
Pepper
Salt

Marinate the chi`cken breasts in the oil, lemon juice, herbs, garlic, salt and pepper for at least 4 hours. Remove the chicken from the marinade and make a split the length of the breast and stuff with the cheese. Place the chicken breast in an ovenproof dish and pour over the marinade, then sprinkle liberally with herbs.

Place in the oven and cook for 45 minutes on Gas mark 6 (425 Deg F, 220 Deg C). Delicious served with Dauphinoise potatoes and a green salad.

Spicy Chicken

Serves 4

Ingredients

2 tbs of oil
4 chicken portions, skinned
1 clove of garlic, peeled and finely chopped
2 large onions, peeled and chopped
1/4 pint (150 ml) of soured cream
1 tbs of paprika
1/4 pint (150ml) of chicken stock
Salt
Pepper

Heat the oil in a casserole dish and fry the onions and garlic slowly for about 5 minutes. They should end up golden colour. When cooking onions to not have the heat up too high as in a manner of seconds the onions can burn. When the onions are cooked add the chicken and paprika and continue to fry for a few minutes. Season, mix in the stock and simmer for 30 minutes.

Just before serving stir in the soured cream. Serve with rice or potatoes.

Coq au Vin

This legendary recipe is another that suits a cold winters' evening. It is traditionally made using red wine from the Burgundy region of France. Burgundy produces some of the finest wines in the world, but they come at a price, usually a high one. If you are on a budget use a robust wine from a cheaper region. It doesn't really matter where you get your coq from.

Serves 4

Ingredients

2oz (50g) butter
3lb (1.5kg) chicken, jointed
10 shallots
1 tbs flour
8 oz (225g) small mushrooms
4 oz (100g) streaky bacon, chopped
1 clove of garlic, crushed
1/2 pint (300ml) red wine
3 tbs brandy
1/4 pint (150ml) chicken stock
1 bouquet garni
1 tbs fresh chopped parsley
Salt
Pepper

Beurre Manie
2 tbs butter
2 tbs flour

Melt the butter in a large casserole dish then fry the chicken pieces for 5 minutes, remove from the dish and set aside. Fry the onions, mushrooms, garlic and bacon for 5 minutes then return the chicken pieces. Pour over the brandy and set alight. Pour in the red wine, stock, bouquet garni, and seasoning, then bring to the boil. Simmer for about 2 hours. Whilst the chicken is simmering prepare the beurre manie as follows. Mix the flour and the butter together to form a soft paste. Then add the beurre manie in small pieces stirring constantly as they are added. Remove the bouquet garni before serving and garnish with the parsley.

Coconut And Chicken Soup

Definitely more than just a soup, really a full meal.

Serves 4

Ingredients

2 tbs of oil
3 chicken breasts
1 pint (600ml) of water
3 oz (75g) of soluble coconut
1/2 tsp of curry powder
2 oz (50g) of fresh ginger
1 tsp of flour
4 tbs of cream, optional
Pepper
Salt

Remove the skin from the chicken, then chop into bite sized pieces. Heat the oil in a large saucepan, and fry the chicken for about 5 minutes, turning frequently to stop it sticking to the pan.

Using a sharp knife remove the outer layer of the ginger and then slice it into thin pieces. Don't make the pieces too small as they are not recommended to be eaten, but should be plucked out of the mixture when served. Add the ginger, curry powder, flour and seasoning to the chicken.

Dissolve the coconut in the water - it is easier if the water is hot. Add the coconut to the other ingredients, bring to the boil, then simmer for 15 to 20 minutes. The cream should be stirred in 5 minutes before serving.

Serve the soup with a side order of rice.

Chicken In Wine

Most chickens love this. They're actually all alcoholics, but not many people realise it because they never drink and drive.

Serves 4

Ingredients

4 chicken pieces
1 glass of red or white wine
2 onions, peeled and chopped
1/2 pint (300ml) of vegetable stock
2 tbs of flour
2 tbs of oil
Pepper
Salt

Put the flour in a dish and roll the chicken pieces in it until they are evenly covered. Heat the oil in a large saucepan then fry the onions for 5 minutes or until they are golden. Fry the chicken pieces for another 5 minutes. Add the stock, onions, salt, pepper and of course the wine, and simmer for 45 minutes.

Chicken Tandoori

Making your own tandoori will cost much less than buying from a take-away or even a supermarket.

Serves 4

Ingredients

4 chicken pieces - breast, thigh or wing
1 tbs of tandoori powder
1 clove of garlic, peeled and finely chopped
1/2 pint (300ml) of plain unsweetened natural yoghurt

Remove the skin from the chicken and make some small incisions in the flesh with a sharp knife - this is to allow the marinade to penetrate deep into the chicken.

Mix the garlic, tandoori powder and yoghurt together, then rub some of the mixture into the incisions. Leave the chicken in the marinade for at least 3 hours, turning occasionally. The longer it is left the more flavour it will gain.

Cook under a medium heat grill for about 20 minutes, spooning on some more marinade at the same time. Turn the chicken over every few minutes to prevent burning.

Chicken Risotto

Risotto dishes are ideal because they are filling, cheap and easy to prepare.

Serves 4

Ingredients

1 oz (25g) of butter
1 onion, peeled and chopped
1 clove of garlic, peeled and finely chopped
6 oz (150g) of chicken, cut into pieces
8 oz (225g) of rice
2 oz (50g) of mushrooms
1 pint (600ml)) of chicken stock

Heat the butter in large a saucepan and fry the chicken pieces for 5 minutes. Remove from the pan and put in a bowl. Fry the onion and garlic for 3 to 4 minutes. Put the rice in a sieve and wash under cold water to remove the starch. Then add the rice to the onions and fry gently for a couple more minutes. Prepare the stock using boiling water, then add a third of it to the saucepan. After the stock has been absorbed by the rice add the rest of the stock and simmer until the rice is cooked. When the rice is cooked add the chicken and mushrooms and cook for a minute or so, to heat them through.

Chicken With Garlic

This title is bit of an understatement, perhaps it should read, garlic with chicken. This is one of those recipes that you might think contains a typographical error, but no, this recipe does require a large quantity of garlic. Traditionally it should use even more, but it has been scaled down a little as garlic is not particularly cheap in this country. Whole cloves are roasted alongside the chicken and when cooked, the cloves can be eaten whole. As they been cooked for so long they loose their strong aroma, however they take on a unique flavour that is delicious.

Serves 4

Ingredients

1 lb (500g) garlic
3 lb (1.5kg) chicken
2 oz (25g) butter
Juice of one lemon
Salt
Pepper

Peel half of the garlic cloves and keep the rest in their skins. Season the chicken inside and out with salt and pepper, then pour the lemon juice over the chicken, again inside and out. Stuff the peeled garlic inside with half of the butter. Smear the remaining butter over the chicken and place with the breastside down in a baking tray. Cook for 30 minutes, then remove from the oven and place the unpeeled garlic cloves around the edge of the chicken and return to the oven. After another hour, turn the chicken onto its back and cook for a further 30 minutes.

When the chicken is cooked remove from the baking tray with the garlic. Serve the chicken with the juices from the pan. The whole garlic cloves can be eaten using your fingers, or spread onto toast. Gas Mark 4 (350 Deg F, 180 Deg C)

Chicken Curry

Serves 4

Ingredients

2 tbs of oil
4 chicken pieces
2 onions, peeled and chopped
2 cloves of garlic, peeled and finely chopped
3 tsp of curry powder
1 tsp of garam masala
2 fresh green chilli peppers, chopped into rings
1 tin of tomatoes (14 oz)
3 whole green cardamom pods
2 tbs of freshly chopped coriander
1 small pot of natural yoghurt
1 to 2 tbs of water
Salt
Pepper

Heat the oil in a large saucepan, then fry the onion and garlic gently for 5 minutes or until they have softened. Add the curry powder, garam masala and chillies, and fry for a couple more minutes. Add the chicken and water and fry for 5 minutes. After this the other ingredients can be added, apart from the yoghurt, which is added 5 minutes before serving. Season to taste. Simmer for 30 to 40 minutes, then serve with rice.

Chicken In Beer

The temptation is always to leave out the chicken from this recipe, but aim for restraint.

Serves 4

Ingredients

2 tbs of oil
4 chicken pieces
1 onion, peeled and chopped
3 carrots, scraped and chopped
1 leek, sliced
4 oz (100g) of mushrooms, sliced
1 large can of your favourite lager
Salt
Pepper

Put the oil in a casserole dish, then fry the onion for 3 to 4 minutes, add the chicken and fry for another 10 minutes. Chuck the rest of the ingredients into the dish then stick into the oven for 1 hour on Gas Mark 5 (400 Deg F, 200 Deg C).

Then drink the rest of the beer, taking care not to get so drunk that you forget to take the chicken out of the oven, or at least switch the oven off.

<u>Lemon Chicken</u>

This recipe is a refreshing change to the more common ways of presenting chicken.

Serves 4

Ingredients

2 tbs of olive oil
4 chicken pieces, preferably breast
Juice of 1 lemon
Pepper

Cut the chicken into small pieces (this allows the lemon to flavour a larger surface area). Heat the oil in a large frying pan then add the chicken, lemon juice and pepper. Fry for 5 minutes, or until the chicken is cooked all the way through, adding more lemon juice before serving if required.

Serve with a salad and pitta or French bread.

Chicken with Mushrooms and Peppers

Serves 4

Ingredients

2 tbs of vegetable oil
4 chicken pieces, breast, leg or thigh, etc
1 green pepper, deseeded and sliced into rings
4 oz (100g) of mushrooms, washed and sliced
1 pint (600ml) of chicken stock
1 onion, peeled and chopped
Salt
Pepper

Heat the oil in a medium sized saucepan, then fry the onions and chicken for about 5 minutes. Stir in the mushrooms, peppers and seasoning and continue to fry gently for another 10 minutes. Pour the chicken stock over the top and simmer for 30 minutes. Serve with potatoes or rice.

Hot Chicken

Serves 4

Ingredients

2 tbs of oil
4 pieces of chicken
1 onion, peeled and chopped
1 green pepper, deseeded and chopped
1 tin of tomatoes (14 oz)
2 tsp of chilli powder
Salt
Pepper

Heat the oil in a large saucepan and fry the onions for 3 to 4 minutes, then add the chilli powder, salt and pepper. Cook for another couple of minutes. Add the chicken and the pepper and cook for about 10 minutes. Then mix in the tomatoes and simmer for 40 minutes, adding a little water if the sauce begins to dry out.

Serve with rice.

Pasta Dishes

There are several things that people associate with Italy, such as Pavarotti, football, bad driving, women who always wear sun-glasses even in the dark, and pasta. The Italians are passionate about most things but food is undoubtedly of great importance and is reflected in everything they do. Pasta is the basis of many Italian dishes and its popularity has spread all over the world. Not only is pasta extremely versatile it is also not particularly fattening, it is only the sauces that are fattening!

Fresh pasta is worth buying if you are cooking pasta for a special occasion as it tastes wonderful. Or alternatively why not buy a pasta machine and make your own fresh pasta.

Pasta is normally served with a sauce, and here the imagination can really run wild. Once you have mastered some of the foundation sauces, such as a basic tomato sauce, you can go on to create your own. When you start to create your own recipes you will find that you gain even more satisfaction.

Cooking Pasta

Allow roughly 2oz (50g) of pasta per person.

Correct cooking of the pasta is essential. After the water has boiled add a good pinch of salt. Long pasta such as spaghetti should be eased gently into a pan making sure that it is not broken. Adding a few of drops of olive oil can prevent the pasta from sticking together. The pasta should be cooked with the lid off, and stirred occasionally.

Normally, dried pasta requires 8 to 10 minutes in boiling water. While it should have some 'bite' to it (al dente), make sure that the pasta is not undercooked, as this could result in indigestion.

If you are cooking fresh pasta it normally only requires 2 or 3 minutes, so watch it carefully. There is a fine line with fresh pasta, with one minute it being perfect, then the next it is over-cooked. Don't always go by the recommended time, taste the pasta whilst it is cooking. If you over-cook your pasta it will stick together and will taste very doughy.

With many recipes that use pasta, there is a certain degree of flexibility with the type of pasta that can be used, although it is a bit tricky trying to produce lasagna with spaghetti.

Pasta Sauces

When producing sauces they should be reduced in volume to increase the intensity of the flavour. Do not boil rapidly but simmer gently.

Tomato Sauce (for pasta dishes)

This is basis of many pasta sauces, so master this before you try anything complicated. Try and use fresh Parmesan that has not been grated as it does not have the same flavour.

Serves 3 to 4

Ingredients

2 tbs of olive oil
1 large onion, peeled and chopped
2 cloves of garlic, peeled and finely chopped
1 tin of tomatoes (14 oz)
1 tbs of tomato purée
2 oz (50g) of Parmesan cheese
6 fresh basil leaves or 1 tsp of dried oregano
Salt
Pepper

Heat the oil in a saucepan, then add the chopped onion and garlic and fry gently for 3 to 4 minutes or until the onions have turned almost translucent. When these have softened, add the tomatoes, purée, herbs, salt and pepper. Cook for another 20 minutes until they have been reduced, then add the cheese if required.

Serve with a pasta of your choice.

Poor Man's Pasta

There are few such recipes that are this simple yet taste so good. This is a perfect dish to repel a hunger attack, and only takes a few minutes to prepare.

Serves 1

Ingredients

4 oz (100g) of any pasta
1/2 clove of garlic finely chopped
2 tbs of olive oil
Salt
Pepper

Cook the pasta according to the instructions on the packet. When the pasta is cooked drain and place in a small serving bowl, add the oil and garlic then season with plenty of black pepper. If you wish to make it a little more exciting add a dash of Tabasco sauce or chilli pepper.

Tomato And Tuna Sauce

Serves 4

Ingredients

2 tbs of olive oil
1 medium onion, peeled and chopped
1 clove of garlic, peeled and finely chopped
1 tin of tomatoes (14oz)
1 tbs of tomato purée
1 tin of tuna
1 tsp of oregano
1 tsp of brown sugar
Salt
Pepper

Heat the oil into a medium sized saucepan and fry the onions and garlic for about 5 minutes. Add the tomatoes, purée, oregano, salt, pepper, sugar. Simmer for about 15 minutes or until the sauce has been reduced, then add the tuna and simmer for a further 5 minutes.

Serve with a pasta of your choice and sprinkle with Parmesan.

Pasta With Sausage

It might seem like an unusual combination but it works well.

Serves 4

Ingredients

4 thick spicy sausages
14 oz (400g) tagliatelle
1 oz (25g) butter
Olive oil
2 oz (50g) finely grated Parmesan
1 clove of garlic, peeled and crushed
1 courgette
2 tbs fresh basil
2 tbs fresh chives
2 tbs fresh parsley
Salt
Pepper

Grill or fry the sausages until cooked then cut into slices. Cook the pasta with a drop of olive oil added to the water to stop it sticking together. Cut the courgette into thin strips so that they look like matchsticks and fry in a little olive oil with the garlic for a couple of minutes. Finely chop the herbs.

When the pasta is cooked, drain and return to the pan. Throw in the cheese, herbs, sausage and butter, mix thoroughly and season. If the cheese has not melted return to the heat for a minute.

Spaghetti Bolognese

There are many variations of the recipe, this is my preferred one.

Serves 4

Ingredients

2 tbs of oil
1 lb (500g) of minced beef
1 onion, peeled and chopped
1 tin of tomatoes (14 oz)
4 oz (100g) of mushrooms, washed and sliced
2 cloves of garlic, finely chopped
1 carrot, grated
2 rashes of bacon, cut into small pieces
Glass of red wine, optional
1 tbs of tomato purée
3/4 pint (350ml) of beef stock
2 tsp of oregano
Salt
Pepper

Put the oil into a large saucepan and heat. Add the onions and garlic, and fry gently for 5 minutes, being careful not to burn them. Add the minced beef and continue frying for a further 10 minutes. Combine the other ingredients.

After your sauce has reduced, which takes around 20 minutes, serve with a pasta of your choice - it doesn't have to be spaghetti.

Tomato and Ham Pasta Sauce

This dish was developed by NASA scientists researching foods for use in space. Tomatoes and ham have long been known to be remarkably resilient to low gravity conditions, and have been eaten on many space missions by hungry astronauts bored of eating out of toothpaste tubes. On earth, tomato and ham pasta sauce is heavy enough not to float around the room while you are preparing it. A fine job done by NASA.

Serves 4

Ingredients

2 tbs of olive oil
1 tin of tomatoes (14 oz)
1 onion, peeled and chopped
4 slices of ham, cut into strips
2 cloves of garlic, peeled and finely chopped
1 tbs of tomato purée
1 glass of red wine, optional
2 tsp of oregano/mixed herbs
Salt
Pepper

Heat the oil in a saucepan and fry the onions and garlic for about 5 minutes. Then add the other ingredients and simmer for 20 minutes. Serve with a pasta of your choice.

Carbonara

I'm not sure if this is the traditional recipe for the dish, but it tastes good to me.

Serves 3 to 4

Ingredients

1 tbs of oil
14 oz (400g) tagliatelle
4 rashers of streaky bacon, cut into small pieces
4 eggs, beaten
3 oz (75g) of grated Parmesan cheese
4 tbs double cream
Lots of fresh black pepper
A pinch of salt

Boil the pasta in a saucepan for about 15 minutes or for however it recommends on the back of the packet. 5 minutes before the pasta is cooked, fry the bacon in the oil for 4 to 5 minutes.

When the pasta is cooked, strain and then return to the pan. Then mix in the cheese, bacon, egg, cream and seasoning. Heat gently for about a minute until the cheese has melted, then serve immediately with more black pepper.

Pasta With Courgette And Bacon Sauce

If you don't have any bacon, slices of ham could be used.

Serves 4

Ingredients

2 tbs of olive oil
1 onion, peeled and chopped
1 clove of garlic, peeled and finely chopped
1 tin of tomatoes (14 oz)
1 tbs of tomato purée
2 rashers of bacon, cut into strips
2 courgettes thinly sliced
2 tsp of oregano/herbes de Provence
Salt
Pepper

Heat the oil in a large saucepan. Add the onion and garlic. Fry for about 3 or 4 minutes, then add the bacon and courgettes. Continue cooking for another 5 minutes, but don't have the heat up too high otherwise the onion will start to burn. A tablespoon of water can be added to help the cooking and to prevent any burning.

When the courgettes have softened add the tomatoes, purée, seasoning and herbs. Simmer the sauce for at least 15 to 20 minutes then serve with pasta and Parmesan or grated cheddar on top.

<u>Lasagna</u>

This is one of everybody's favourite Italian dishes. See the vegetarian section for an alternative recipe.

Serves 4

Ingredients

2 tbs of oil
1 large onion, peeled and chopped
2 cloves of garlic, peeled and finely chopped
1 lb (500g) of minced beef
1 tin of tomatoes (14 oz)
1/4 pint (150ml) of beef stock
2 tbs of tomato purée
2 tsp of oregano
Salt
Pepper
1 packet of lasagna (the "no pre-cooking required type")

For the sauce:

1 oz (25g) of butter
2 oz (50g) of flour
1 pint (600ml) of milk
6 oz (150g) of cheese, grated

After heating the oil in a large saucepan add the onion and garlic and cook for 5 minutes. Add the mince and cook thoroughly. Then add the tomatoes, oregano, beefstock, tomato purée and seasoning. After bringing to the boil, simmer for 15 to 20 minutes.

While the meat sauce is reducing, prepare the cheese sauce. Melt the butter in a saucepan and then add the flour, stirring constantly. Remove from the heat and add the milk in stages. If the milk is added in one go, you end up with lumps (in the sauce). After adding the milk, bring to the boil and add the cheese, saving a bit for the top. Then simmer for 3 or 4 minutes; the sauce should now begin to thicken.

OK, so your sauce has not thickened: don't panic! Try adding a bit more flour, but sieve if first if you can. Lumpiness can be rectified by pouring the mixture through a sieve.

Find a shallow baking dish and grease it, then add a layer of meat sauce followed by a layer of lasagna, followed by a layer of cheese sauce. Continue this formation until you have used up your mixtures, making sure you finish with the cheese sauce. As well as sprinkling cheese on top, fresh tomato can be added.

Bake on the middle shelf of a pre-heated oven at Gas Mark 6 (425 Deg F, 220 Deg C) for 30 to 40 minutes.

Parsley And Pasta

Serves 2

Ingredients

6 oz (150g) of wholemeal pasta shells
1 blob of butter or margarine
1 or 2 oz (25 or 50g) of cheddar cheese, grated
Lots of fresh parsley, roughly chopped
Salt
Pepper

Boil the pasta according to the instructions on the packet, then drain. Add the butter and allow it to melt. Add the salt, pepper, cheese and parsley, and toss until evenly distributed, then serve immediately.

Pizza

Pizza Marguerita

This is the basic pizza, the 1.6L model with no stereo. If you want to design your own, begin with this and add your own toppings.

Serves 1

Ingredients

1 pizza base
Tomato purée
1 tsp of olive oil
1 oz (25g) of grated cheese
Pinch of oregano
Pepper

Spread some tomato purée on top of the pizza base. A thin layer will do - if you put too much on, your pizza will become soggy. Place the cheese on top, season, add the herbs and pour on the oil. Bake in the oven until the cheese turns a golden brown colour. It should take roughly 15 minutes on Gas Mark 7 (450 Deg F, 230 Deg C), or until the cheese turns golden brown.

Pizza Lira

The Lira is one of the most exciting currencies in the world: if you have enough Lire to buy a pizza, you are a Lire millionaire. The Pizza Lira is no less exciting, but it won't make you rich.

Serves 1

Ingredients

1 pizza base
Tomato purée
1 slice of ham
2 medium sized mushrooms, washed and sliced
1 oz (25g) of grated cheese
1 tsp of oil
Pinch of oregano
Pepper

Spread some tomato purée on the pizza base, then add the ham. If the slice is too large, cut it into a more usable size. Add a layer of mushrooms and cover with cheese. Season, add the oregano and cook as above recipe.

Pizza Perugia

Serves 1

Ingredients

1 pizza base
Tomato purée
1 tsp of oil
1 oz (25g) of grated cheese
2 oz (50g) of tuna
2 to 3 onion rings
Pinch of oregano
Pepper

Spread some tomato purée on the pizza base. Place the tuna on the purée, then the onion rings and finally the cheese. Season, add the oregano and oil and cook as above.

Fish

Most fish that is available is caught commercially and unless you fish for yourself or have friends who do so you are unlikely to be able to obtain locally caught fish. If you are lucky and live near the coast you may be able to buy freshly caught fish and shellfish directly from the fishermen.

Fish can either be classified as fresh-water or sea-water or as white fish or oily fish.

Examples of white fish are cod, plaice, haddock, skate, mullet and monk fish, examples of oily fish include sardines, herring, mackerel and salmon.

Due to the muscle fibre structure in fish they are naturally tender. Bearing this in mind fish need careful cooking. Fish should be eaten as soon after cooking as possible as they tend to dry out.

Fish are particularly nutritious and low in fat so they are ideal as part of a diet. They make a good source of protein, calcium and phosphorous and oily fish contain valuable vitamin D. Although many fish are far from cheap, certain fish such as herrings and fresh mackerel are extremely good value.

Some sea food restaurants on the Mediterranean have fish tanks from which you can choose a particular fish, then in 15 minutes it will be sitting on your plate. As I was walking past one restaurant in which such a practice took place a chosen fish made the dash for freedom and belly flopped onto the pavement. Trying to catch a slippery fish on a crowded pavement is not easy, but it didn't get far! For some this closeness to the potential food is a little off-putting, and I'm sure that if a restaurant had an attached field with a herd of cows from which you could choose a steak there would be an increase in the number of vegetarians.

If a recipe uses a whole fish it will need cleaning. Rather than give it a bubble bath, the head, gills and innards have to be removed. Normally fish come already 'cleaned', but, if they don't, ask the fishmonger to do it for you.

Look for the following qualities when choosing fish:

- It should not smell.

- The eyes should be bright and full. If the fish is not so fresh the eyes will be dull.

- The gills should be slime-free, clean and shiny.

- If you press a fresh fish with your finger, the flesh should spring back up.

Fresh fish should be eaten on the day of purchase. Frozen fish does not tend to have as full a flavour as fresh fish. It is, however, useful to keep a couple of cod fillets in the freezer as they can be cooked fairly quickly and easily.

There are several ways of cooking fish, depending on the type of fish and what sort of flavour is required. These are the most popular methods: baking, poaching, frying and grilling.

Baked Mackerel

Serves 2

Ingredients

2 mackerel
2 tsp of mustard
2 tsp of vinegar
2 tbs of water

Clean the mackerel, then score across two or three times on each side. Sprinkle with mustard, vinegar and water. Put the fish in a greased baking tin and bake for 15 to 20 minutes on Gas Mark 5 (400 Deg F, 200 Deg C).

Baked Fish With Ginger

Serves 1 to 2, depending on size of fish

Ingredients

1 whole fish, such as red snapper, cleaned
1 clove of garlic, peeled and finely chopped
1 tsp of soy sauce
Juice of 1 lemon
1 oz (25g) of fresh ginger, peeled and thinly sliced
Tin foil

Place the fish on a piece of foil. Mix the lemon juice, soy sauce, garlic and ginger together and pour over the fish. Seal the fish in the foil and bake in the oven for 45 minutes at Gas Mark 5 (400 Deg F, 200 Deg C).

Halibut Casserole

Serves 4

Ingredients

2 tbs oil
4 halibut steaks
1 onion, peeled and chopped
1/2 pint (300ml) white wine
1 garlic clove, peeled and crushed
1 tbs cornflour
8 oz (225g) tomatoes, skinned, deseeded and chopped
1 tbs tomato purée
Salt
Pepper

Heat the oil in a casserole dish. Add the onion and garlic and fry gently for 3 to 4 minutes. Stir in the cornflour, tomatoes, tomato purée and the wine. Bring slowly to the boil stirring constantly then add the fish and simmer for 10 minutes or until the fish is cooked. The perfect accompaniment is mashed potato.

Oatmeal Herrings

Oatmeal herrings are a more healthy alternative to plain white ones, though they go rather soggy in water.

Serves 4

Ingredients

Vegetable oil
4 fresh herrings
4 tbs oatmeal
Salt
Pepper

A sharp knife is needed. Clean the herrings, removing the heads, tails and fins. Remove the innards by making a slit along the under side of the fish and pull them out with your fingers or use a knife. Lay the fish on a board face down and flatten, this makes it easier to remove the backbone. Turn the fish over and pull out the bone. Rinse the fish under running water then pat dry with kitchen paper. Mix the oatmeal, salt and pepper together then coat the fish in the mixture. Fry in hot oil until both sides are brown. Serve with lemon wedges.

Grilled Cod

Serves 1

Ingredients

1 cod steak
Butter
Pepper
Salt

Brush the fish with a little butter, season, and grill for about 10 minutes, according to the size and thickness of the fish. Turn occasionally.

If you like a bit more flavour, squeeze some lemon or lime juice on top. Serve with potatoes or rice and fresh vegetables.

Baked Fish In Wine

Serves 2

Ingredients

2 cod steaks
1 onion, peeled and cut into rings
1 glass of wine, red or white
Pepper
Salt

Put the fish and onions in a shallow baking dish, season and pour the wine over the top. Bake in the oven for 35 minutes at Gas Mark 5 (400 Deg F, 200 Deg C).

<u>Kedgeree</u>

Serves 4

Ingredients

1 egg
8 oz (225g) of rice
8 oz (225g) of smoked haddock fillet
2 oz (50g) of butter
Juice of 1 lemon
Pepper
Salt

Cook the fish by baking it in the oven for 25 minutes. Then remove from the oven and 'flake fish', removing all bones and skin. Boil the rice in according to the instructions on the packet.

Drain and rinse the rice in boiling water - this gets rid of most of the starch. Hard boil the egg by boiling it for 10 minutes. Then cool, remove the shell and chop into pieces.

Melt the butter in a saucepan and add the fish. Cook the fish for 3 to 4 minutes to reheat it. Stir in the lemon juice, chopped egg, seasoning and rice and serve immediately. Garnish with fresh parsley.

Fish Cakes

Serves 4

Ingredients

8 oz (225g) cooked cod
8 oz (225g) mashed potato
1 oz (25g) melted butter
1 egg, beaten
Dried breadcrumbs
1 tbs chopped parsley
Salt
Pepper

Remove the skin and bones from the fish and flake. Mix the fish, potato, parsley, butter, salt and pepper together. Shape into 6-8 cakes by hand. Dip the fish cakes into the egg mixture then roll in the breadcrumbs. Shallow fry in hot fat until they are a golden brown on both sides.

Baked Trout

Serves 2

Ingredients

2 small trout, cleaned
1 onion, peeled and finely chopped
1 carrot, peeled and finely chopped
1 clove of garlic, peeled and finely chopped
1 oz (25g) of flaked almonds
1/2 oz (15g) of butter
Salt
Pepper

Melt the butter in a frying pan, then add the onion, carrot, and garlic. Fry for about 5 minutes. Place each trout on a piece of tin foil, making sure the foil is big enough to completely wrap the fish. Divide the vegetables between the two fish, placing the vegetables on the top and the sides of the fish, sprinkle with the almonds, season, then seal up the tin foil parcels.

Bake in the oven for about 20 minutes or Gas Mark 5 (200 Deg C, 400 Deg F).

Serve with potatoes, rice or salad.

Grilled Sardines

Fresh sardines are a favourite in France. In June, they have special parties to celebrate this little fish called Sardinières. The sardines are served grilled with plenty of salt and lemon. If the sardines are small enough they are not normally gutted, but if they large then have the fishmonger gut them for you as this is a fiddly process.

Serves 4

Ingredients

16 small sardines
Olive oil
Salt
Lemon

Pre-heat the grill to its hottest setting, then place the sardines on the grill pan. Brush with a little oil, sprinkle with salt and cook for 4 minutes on each side. They taste even better if they are barbecued. Serve with lemon juice and a simple salad, bread and wine.

Cod And Onion Bake

Serves 4

Ingredients

4 pieces of cod or any white fish
1 large onion, peeled and sliced into separate rings
3 sliced tomatoes
2 oz (50g) of butter

This is an easy dish to prepare that should take no more than 5 minutes. Put the fish and onion into an ovenproof dish with the butter, and bake for 20 minutes on Gas Mark 5 (400 Deg F, 200 Deg C). Add the sliced tomatoes and cook for a further 10 minutes.

Serve with potatoes and fresh vegetables.

Vegetarian Dishes

Over the past decade the interest in vegetarian food has escalated such that it is usual for most people to eat certain meat-free recipes in their normal diet. Whatever the reason for becoming a vegetarian it is a misconception that vegetarian cooking is boring. The people that say this are the sort of people that eat pie and chips every night and think that a courgette is some sort of American car. I am certainly not a vegetarian, but enjoy vegetarian food. There is great scope for experimentation with vegetables. Try to get away from the meat and two veg mentality, be bold, you might find yourself pleasantly surprised.

Piperade

This is one of those dishes that is quick and easy to prepare and is suitable for a light lunch or supper. The dish originates from the Basque country. Add a pinch of paprika if you want it with a little bite.

Serves 4

Ingredients

6 eggs
2 tbs butter
2 red peppers, deseeded
2 green peppers, deseeded
2 cloves of garlic, peeled and chopped
6 tomatoes, skinned
1 tbs chopped fresh basil
Salt
Pepper

Cut the peppers into strips and chop the tomatoes. Heat the butter in a frying pan and cook the peppers for 10 minutes. Add the chopped tomatoes, garlic, basil and seasoning and cook until the tomatoes are almost to a pulp. Take care that the vegetables do not burn. Whilst the vegetables are cooking, beat the eggs in a basin. When the vegetables are ready add the eggs. Stir the mixture until it thickens, but do not let the eggs set completely. This dish is traditionally served with slices of fried ham.

Stuffed Marrow

Serves 4

Ingredients

3 tbs of oil
1 large marrow
1 onion, peeled and chopped
8 oz (225g) of rice
1 tin of tomatoes (14 oz)
3 oz (75g) of mushrooms, chopped
Bunch of parsley
1 tsp of mixed herbs
Salt
Pepper

Wash the marrow then cut a lengthways slice off the top. Using a large spoon remove the seeds. This should create a substantial hollow. Sprinkle the inside of the marrow with salt then turn it upside down.

Heat the oil in a large frying pan and fry the onion for about 5 minutes. Add the rice and cook for another couple of minutes. Now add the other ingredients except the marrow, adding a few tablespoons of water if needed. Cook for 15 minutes. Rinse the marrow with water and then shake dry. Fill the marrow with the contents of the frying pan then replace the top and wrap in foil. Bake on the middle shelf of the oven at Gas Mark 4 (350 Deg F, 180 Deg C) for about 80 minutes. It might take longer depending on the size of the marrow. Once a skewer can pass easily through the flesh of the marrow it is ready to be served.

Aubergine Bake

Serves 4

Ingredients

2 tbs of oil
1 large aubergine, thinly sliced
2 onions, peeled and chopped
2 cloves of garlic, chopped
5 oz (125g) pot of natural yoghurt
1 tin of tomatoes (14 oz)
1 tbs of tomato purée
1 tsp of dried oregano
3 oz (75g) of grated cheddar cheese
1 oz (25g) of white breadcrumbs
Salt
Pepper

Heat the oil in a frying pan and add the aubergine slices. It is best to cook it in stages because only the bottom of the pan needs to be covered at any one time. Fry the aubergine until it has softened and slightly browned, then place on kitchen paper to absorb the oil. After cooking all the aubergine, remove it and fry the onion and garlic for 5 minutes.

The next stage is to add the tomato, tomato purée, oregano and seasoning. Bring to the boil, then simmer for 10 minutes before stirring in the yoghurt.

Using a greased ovenproof dish, arrange the aubergine then the tomato sauce in alternate layers. Continue this until the top layer is of aubergine. Cover the top with breadcrumbs and cheese.

Bake at Gas Mark 4 (350 Deg F, 180 Deg C), for around 30 minutes. Serve with rice or potatoes.

Jacket Potato

It is important to use old potatoes - new ones are not suitable.
This also applies to roast potatoes.

Serves 1

Ingredients

1 large potato

After viciously stabbing your potato with a sharp implement (preferably a fork), bung in the oven for about 60 minutes on Gas Mark 7 (450 Deg F, 230 Deg C).

Test the potato with a skewer or a knife to see if it is cooked in the middle. The skewer should pass easily through the potato.

Jacket Potato With Cheese And Onion

This is another way of cooking jacket potatoes, but it takes a little more time to prepare and to eat.

Serves 1

Ingredients

1 large potato
2 oz (50g) of cheddar cheese, grated
1 onion
1 tbs of milk
A nob of butter

Follow the instructions for the above recipe. Slice the cooked potato in half. Scoop the potato out of the skin using a teaspoon and place the contents into a mixing bowl. Try not to make a hole in the skins because you'll need them later.

Add a tablespoon of milk and a nob of butter and mash. Cut the onion up into pieces and fry for 3 to 4 minutes. Add the onion to the potato and mix together. Then spoon the potato back into the jackets, cover with cheese and cook for another 15 minutes or so. If the cheese starts to burn cover the potato with a piece of tin foil.

Macaroni Cheese

This another of my favourite recipes. If you don't have any macaroni use pasta shells.

Serves 4

Ingredients

6 oz (150g) of macaroni
6 oz (150g) of grated cheddar cheese
2 large tomatoes
3/4 pint (350ml) of milk
1 oz (25g) of flour or cornflour
1 oz (25g) of butter

Melt the butter in a saucepan and mix in the flour. Gradually add the milk, stirring constantly to prevent lumps. Bring to the boil, add the cheese, then leave to simmer for 3 to 4 minutes.

Now cook the macaroni according to the instructions on the packet. When this is done, drain and mix with the cheese sauce. Put into a baking dish, top with sliced tomatoes and more cheese. Grill until browned.

Vegetable Bake

Serves 4

Ingredients

2 tbs of oil
1 onion, peeled
1 clove of garlic
1 courgette
1 small tin of sweetcorn
1 tin of tomatoes (14 oz)
1 oz (25g) of mushrooms
2 oz (50g) of cheddar
2 slices of bread
1 vegetarian Oxo cube
Mixed herbs
A slosh of red wine, if available
Salt
Pepper

Pre-heat the oven to 150 Deg C (300 Deg F, Gas Mark 2). Slice the onion, garlic, courgette and mushrooms, and lightly fry in the oil for 5 minutes. Add the sweetcorn, tomatoes, herbs, seasoning and wine. Mix the Oxo cube with a cup of water and add to the pan, simmer for about 10 minutes.

If there is a food processor around, use it to turn the bread into breadcrumbs. Otherwise just tear the bread into oblivion with your bare (but clean) hands. Grate the cheese.

Pour the vegetables into a casserole dish and cover with breadcrumbs and cheese. Put into the oven for 10 to 20 minutes, until the breadcrumbs have gone crispy and the cheese has melted.

Alternatively, serve without breadcrumbs and cheese as a sauce for pasta or rice.

Cabbage Parcels

Serves 2

Ingredients

6 large cabbage leaves
8 oz (225g) of spinach
6 oz (150g) of cooked rice
2 oz (50g) of butter
4 oz (100g) of grated cheddar cheese
1 egg yolk
1/2 pint (300ml) of vegetable stock

First, simmer the spinach in a little water for 5 minutes, then drain and put aside. Simmer the cabbage leaves for about two minutes and remove from the water.

Melt the butter and add the chopped onion together with the rice, spinach, cheese, and seasoning. Bind with the egg yolk.

When thoroughly mixed, put a heaped spoonful of it onto each of the cabbage leaves, and wrap into parcels. Place the parcels in an ovenproof dish and pour the stock on top.

Cover with foil and bake for 30 minutes at Gas Mark 4 (350 Deg F, 180 Deg C).

Bubble And Squeak

This requires scraping the leftovers from the previous day/week out of the bin-liner, then melting it down to a substance slightly less chewy than industrial glue.

Ingredients

2 tbs of oil
Mashed potato
Greens or Brussels sprouts
Egg
Whatever else has got stuck to it overnight

Kill any ingredients that are still moving. Fry the mixture until it smells edible, then eat if you dare. This meal may reproduce itself day after day.

Potato And Tomato Cake

Serves 4

Ingredients

2 tbs of oil
2 lb (1kg) of 'old' potatoes
Tin of tomatoes (14oz)
1 onion, peeled and finely chopped
Salt
Pepper

Heat the oil in a pan and fry the onion gently for 10 minutes then add the tomato, salt and pepper. Keep the heat low and simmer for about 20 minutes so the sauce reduces to a thick liquid. Whilst the sauce is reducing boil the potatoes until they are soft enough to mash. When they get to this stage mash them. Gradually mix the sauce with the mashed potatoes. When all the sauce is added, spoon the mixture out onto a serving plate and mould into the shape of a cake. Eat hot or cold.

Vegetable Stir Fry

Those fortunate enough to possess a wok will find Oriental cooking a lot easier than those stuck with the indignity of a frying pan. If you do have to use a frying pan, use the biggest one you have. The wok is one of my most used kitchen accessories. Its use does not have to be confined to Oriental cooking.

It is up to you what to put into a stir fry, though it is often a good way of using up any spare vegetables that are lurking at the back of your cupboard. Experiment with exotic vegetables, oils and pastes.

Serves 4

Ingredients

2 tbs of oil
1 onion, peeled and chopped
1 red pepper, deseeded and chopped
1 green pepper, deseeded and chopped
1 carrot, cut into thin strips
1 clove of garlic, peeled and finely chopped
1 tin of bamboo shoots
1 tin of water chestnuts
1 pack of fresh bean sprouts
2 tbs of soy sauce
Salt
Pepper

Pour the oil into your wok, then when the oil is hot, ie when it is smoking (try not to set fire to the kitchen in the process), add the onion and garlic, and fry for 5 minutes. If you are using water chestnuts, cook these first as they take the longest to cook, and are nicer when they are slightly crispy. Add the soy sauce, seasoning, and other vegetables except for the beansprouts.

After frying the vegetables for about 5 to 10 minutes, add the beansprouts and cook for a couple more minutes. It is important to keep the beansprouts firm. Serve with rice.

Lentil Curry

Serves 2

Ingredients

2 tbs oil
4 oz (100g) of lentils soaked in cold water for 1 hour
1/2 pint (300ml) of vegetable stock
4 carrots, scraped and chopped
1 onion, peeled and chopped
1 courgette, sliced
1 leek, sliced
1 tbs of curry powder
2 fresh tomatoes sliced
Salt
Pepper

Boil the lentils for about 7 minutes and then strain. Heat the oil in a large saucepan, then fry the onions and curry powder for 5 minutes. Add the other vegetables and fry for another 5 minutes. Then pour in the stock and lentils, bring to the boil, and simmer for an hour. Season.

<u>Ratatouille</u>

This traditional Provençal recipe can really be made from whatever vegetables are available. Tinned tomatoes are cheaper than buying fresh ones (except in the summer when fresh ones are more affordable).

Serves 4

Ingredients

2 tbs of oil
1 tin of tomatoes (14 oz)
1 onion, peeled and finely chopped
2 cloves of garlic, peeled and finely chopped
1 small aubergine, chopped
1 red pepper, deseeded and chopped
1 courgette, sliced
1 lemon, quartered
2 tsp of herbes de Provence
1 bay leaves
A glass of red wine, water or tomato juice, optional
Pepper
Salt

While you are preparing the other vegetables, place the pieces of aubergine on a plate and sprinkle them with salt.

After preparing the other vegetables, wash the aubergine pieces then dry them with kitchen paper.

Heat the oil in a large saucepan. Fry the onions and garlic for about 5 minutes, then add the courgette, the aubergines and the peppers. Cook for about 5 minutes before adding the tomatoes, lemon, and other ingredients. Bring to the boil and simmer for 30 minutes.

<u>Vegetable Curry</u>

Trying to produce the perfect curry is not easy unless you have those authentic accompaniments such as wall to wall mauve carpet, with high backed carpeted chairs, background Sitar music, steaming hot towels that enable one to have a quick wash at the end of the meal and not forgetting half the local rugby team exposing themselves on the table next to you. It's enough to make you choke on your poppadom, but the food is great.

If you are interested in cooking Indian food then buy a book on the subject as I am not going to attempt to explain the complexities that are involved, such as grinding your own spices. For now I have included a basic curry that uses readily available ingredients and pre-ground curry powder.

Serves 4

Ingredients

2 tbs of oil
4 potatoes, diced into 1 inch (2.5cm) cubes
1 sliced leek
1 tin of tomatoes (14 oz)
2 sliced courgettes
1 onion, peeled and chopped
2 cloves of garlic, peeled and finely chopped
1 small pot of natural yoghurt
1 tbs of Madras curry powder
1 dried red chilli
1/2 pint (300ml) of vegetable stock
Any spare vegetables
1 to 2 tbs of water

Heat the oil in a large saucepan then fry the onion, garlic and curry powder for 5 minutes or until they have softened.

Add the other ingredients, except the yoghurt, bring to the boil, and simmer for 40 minutes or more. Stir in the yoghurt 5 minutes before serving.

Whilst the curry is simmering taste it to see if it is to the strength required. If it is not hot enough for your asbestos-lined mouth just add more curry powder.

Serve with rice, preferably pilau or basmati.

Vegetable Kebabs

You do not have to stick to the vegetables suggested in this recipe.

Serves 2

Ingredients

1 oz (25g) of butter
1 green pepper, deseeded and cut into pieces
1 courgette, cut into chunks
1 small onion, peeled and quartered
2 tomatoes, quartered
4 mushrooms, halved or quartered
Salt
Pepper

Thread all the vegetables onto a couple of skewers and daub them with butter, then grill for about 15 minutes.

For a different flavour try adding a tablespoon of runny honey or a dash of soy sauce whilst grilling.

Serve with rice.

Fruit and Nut Pasta

The pine nuts and the sultanas is an unusual combination but you will find it delicious.

Serves 4

Ingredients

8 tbs of olive oil
14 oz (400g) of pasta
2 cloves of garlic, peeled and finely chopped
2 oz (50g) of sultanas
2 oz (50g) of pine kernels
Pepper

Cook the pasta of your choice according to the instructions on the packet.

Drain the pasta and place in a serving bowl. Pour the oil over the pasta then stir in the garlic, pine kernels and sultanas. Season using lots of fresh ground pepper then serve immediately. Parmesan can be added on top if required.

Crunchy Rice

This recipe is best cooked in a large wok, but a saucepan or a dustbin lid will do.

Serves 2 to 4

Ingredients

2 tbs of oil
2 cups of wholemeal rice
4 cups of water
1 green pepper, deseeded and chopped
1 small tin of sweetcorn
1 onion, peeled and chopped
1 oz (25g) of mushrooms, sliced
1 clove of garlic, peeled and finely chopped
2 oz (50g) of walnuts
1 vegetarian Oxo cube
1 tbs fresh chopped parsley
Salt
Pepper

Heat the oil in a large frying pan or wok, then fry the onions and garlic for between 4 and 5 minutes. Add the mushrooms, green pepper and sweetcorn and fry for another couple of minutes. Next add the uncooked rice and about four cups of water. Sprinkle the Oxo cube over and stir frequently. Simmer for about 20 minutes, depending on the type of rice used. Add more water if necessary to stop the rice from drying out.

If the rice is soft when pinched then it is cooked. Add the walnuts a couple of minutes before removing from the heat. Season with salt and pepper and garnish with the parsley.

Lasagna

You can use a meat substitute with this recipe, called silken tofu. It sounds like a Greek island, but it tastes a bit better than that. If you can find some, prepare in the same way as the meat lasagna, substituting the meat for tofu.

Serves 4

Ingredients

2 tbs of oil
1 large onion, peeled and chopped
1 red pepper, deseeded and chopped
1 green pepper, deseeded and chopped
1 clove of garlic, peeled and finely chopped
1 leek finely chopped
2 courgettes finely sliced
1 tin of tomatoes (14 oz)
2 tbs of tomato purée
2 tsp of oregano
1 packet of lasagna (no pre-cooking required type)
Salt
Pepper

For the cheese sauce:

1 oz (25g) of butter
2 oz (50g) of flour
1 pint (600ml) of milk
6 oz (150g) of cheese, grated

Heat the oil in a large saucepan and add the onion and garlic. Cook for 5 minutes, then stir in the leek, peppers and courgette, fry gently for another 3 minutes or so. Add the tomatoes, purée, oregano and seasoning. Bring to the boil then simmer for a further 20 minutes. While the vegetable sauce is simmering prepare the cheese sauce.

Melt the butter in a saucepan and add the flour, stirring constantly. Remove from the heat and add the milk in stages. Then bring to the boil and add the cheese, saving a bit for the top. Simmer for 3 or 4 minutes. Add more flour if the sauce refuses to thicken.

Grease a shallow baking dish, then add a layer of tomato sauce, a layer of lasagna, a layer of cheese sauce, a layer of lasagna, and so on, making sure to end up with cheese sauce on top. Sprinkle the loose cheese on top.

Bake in a pre-heated oven for around 25 minutes at Gas Mark 6 (425 Deg F, 220 Deg C).

Hot Vegetable Stew

This is yet another recipe that can be altered to taste and what vegetables are available. If you are not a fan of hot food you can always omit the spices.

Serves 4

Ingredients

2 tbs of oil
1 onion, peeled and chopped
2 cloves of garlic, peeled and finely chopped
1 pepper, deseeded and sliced
2 courgettes sliced
1 leek, sliced
1 tin (14 oz) of tomatoes
3 potatoes, peeled and diced
Small can of sweetcorn
4 oz (100g) of cooked green lentils
1 green chilli pepper, chopped
Dash of Tabasco sauce
1 pint (600ml) vegetable stock
2 tsp of mixed herbs
Salt
Pepper

Heat the oil in a large casserole dish, then fry the onions and garlic adding the chilli and Tabasco, for 3 to 4 minutes. Add the courgettes, leeks and peppers and gently fry for a further 10 minutes. Then add the stock and the remaining ingredients. Bring to the boil and simmer for 30 minutes.

Stuffed Peppers

Having dinner with friends one evening near Cassis on the French coast the host brought out a wonderful platter of stuffed vegetables, including peppers, tomatoes, aubergines, tomatoes and courgettes. Mediterranean cuisine is a wonderful concoction of influences. North Africa is only a short hop away and the area is heavily influenced by countries such as Tunisia, Morocco and Algeria. Anyway, back to the stuffed peppers.

Serves 4

Ingredients

2 tbs of olive oil
4 peppers
1 onion, peeled and chopped
1 clove of garlic, peeled and finely chopped
1 tin (14 oz) tomatoes
2 tsp of tomato purée
4 oz (100g) mushrooms
Glass of red wine
1 tbs of chopped parsley
1 tsp of chopped rosemary
Dash of lemon juice
2 tbs of breadcrumbs
Salt
Pepper

Cut the tops off the peppers and remove the seeds, then place in boiling water for 3 to 4 minutes. Remove and plunge in cold water.

Heat the oil in a large saucepan, then gently fry the onion and garlic for a few minutes. Add the other ingredients, bring to the boil and then simmer for 10 minutes. Fill the peppers with the mixture, replace the lid of the pepper and bake in the oven for 35 minutes on Gas Mark 6 (425 Deg F, 220 Deg C).

Remember to preheat the oven.

French Beans With Garlic

If you have runner beans they can be used instead, provided you can catch them first.

Serves 4

Ingredients

1 lb (500g) French beans
1 clove of garlic, peeled and finely chopped
1 oz (25g) butter
Salt
Pepper

Top and tail the beans then cut in two. Place the beans in a pan of salted boiling water and cook for 10 minutes or until tender. It is important that they are not over-cooked as they will lose their colour and flavour. When cooked, drain the beans. Heat the butter in the pan and let it melt, but don't let it burn. Add the garlic and cook for a minute then add the beans and season. Stir the beans to make sure they are evenly coated before serving.

Courgettes can be cooked in a similar way, except they do not need to be boiled, they can be fried gently in the butter with the garlic.

Okra And Tomatoes

Okra are also referred to 'ladies' fingers' which whilst not necessarily whetting the appetite is a mite better than 'ladies' toes'.

Serves 4

Ingredients

3 tbs olive oil
1 lb (500g) okra
1 lb (500g) tomatoes
1 small onion, peeled and chopped
1 clove of garlic, peeled and crushed
1 tbs lemon juice
1 tsp garam masala
2 tbs chopped coriander
Salt
Pepper

Trim the thick ends of the okra and then cut them in half. Place the tomatoes in boiling water for 1 minute. Remove the tomato skins and quarter.

Heat the oil in a large frying pan, then cook the onion for 5 minutes. Add the okra and cook for a further five minutes. Stir in the other ingredients, except for the coriander and cook until the okra is tender. Garnish with the coriander.

Dauphinoise Potatoes

If I could only eat potatoes cooked one way it would have to be this. The combination of potatoes and cream is delicious. They go particularly well with dishes such as hot vegetable stew or chicken in beer.

Serves 4

Ingredients

2 lb (1kg) 'old' potatoes, peeled and thinly sliced
1 large onion, peeled and thinly sliced
2 cloves of garlic, peeled and crushed
1/2 pint (300ml) double cream
2 oz (50g) butter
Nutmeg
Salt
Pepper

Grease the base and sides of an oven-proof dish, then put alternate layers of onion, potato, garlic, slices of butter, cream, salt, pepper and grated nutmeg in the dish. Finish with a layer of potatoes. Place in a pre-heated oven at Gas Mark 5 (400 Deg F, 200 Deg C) for about 1½ hours. If required, freshly grated cheese such as Gruyère or Parmesan can be added.

N.B Only a small amount of nutmeg is used on each layer, the flavour must not be overpowering.

Supper And Snacks

There are certain times when you will not be in the mood for cooking an elaborate meal or you might just fancy something light and quick and easy to prepare. It is often the case of seeing what ingredients you have and creating a recipe from what is available (this does not mean combining cornflakes and mango chutney).

Ham And Eggs

This a perfect supper or lunch dish, that takes only a few minutes to prepare.

Serves 4

Ingredients

4 large eggs
4 slices of ham
Tin of chopped tomatoes (14oz)
Herbes du Provence
Salt
Pepper

Heat the oven to its maximum temperature. Pour the tomatoes into a baking dish then roll up the slices of ham and place on top of the tomato. Break the eggs carefully on top of the ham, sprinkle with the herbs and season. Bake until the eggs are cooked. Serve with hot buttered toast. I always serve this at Christmas using leftovers from a ham. It makes a refreshing change from the usual Christmas fare.

B.L.T.

Otherwise known as a bacon, lettuce and tomato sandwich.

Serves 1

Ingredients

Butter
3 slices of bread
2 rashers of bacon
A lettuce leaf or two
1 tomato
Salt
Pepper

Remove the crusts from the bread, then slice the tomato. Grill the bacon and the bread. Butter the toast, then place a bit of lettuce, some tomato and a rasher of bacon on it. Put a slice of toast on top and then make up another layer as before. Finish with the last piece of toast on top, then cut diagonally across. Add a dash of salt and pepper if required.

To stop the B.L.T. from falling apart you could try skewering it with a cocktail stick. But under no circumstances should you swallow the cocktail stick in your haste to eat your masterpiece - they are not particularly palatable.

Egg Hubble-Bubble

Serves 1 to 2

Ingredients

4 potatoes, boiled
Any other vegetables
Butter or margarine
Cheese
4 eggs, lightly beaten and seasoned

Dice the potato, then fry it with any other vegetables you may have (eg mushrooms, tomato, peas) in butter or margarine. When cooked, pour in the eggs and sprinkle with grated cheese. Cook very slowly with a plate or lid over the top, until the eggs are set.

Mini Roasts With Bacon

Serves 4

Ingredients

2 lb (1kg) 'old' potatoes
6 rashers of bacon
Herbs du Provence
Olive oil
Salt
Pepper

Peel the potatoes and cut into one inch cubes. Cut the bacon into small pieces. Place the potatoes in a large baking tin with the bacon, sprinkle with herbs and then season. Baste with oil so that all the potatoes are evenly coated.

Place in a pre-heated oven Gas Mark 6, (425 Deg F, 225 Deg C) and cook until crisp.

Quiche

For this recipe an 8 inch (20cm) flan dish and a rolling pin are needed.

Once the basic technique of making a quiche is mastered, limitless combinations of this classic French dish can be produced. Many people are put off preparing a quiche because it involves making pastry, but it is not as hard as many people think.

Short Crust Pastry

Ingredients for pastry

8 oz (225g) of plain flour
2 oz (50g) of lard
2 oz (50g) of margarine/butter
2/3 tbs of water
A pinch of salt

After sieving the flour and the salt add the lard and butter. The fat is easier to rub in if it is cut into little cubes. The term 'rubbing in' is the procedure in which, using the fingertips, the flour and the fat are combined to produce a consistency of fine bread crumbs.

After rubbing in, add some water a little at a time. The water is needed to bind the mixture together, but be careful not to add so much that the pastry becomes sticky. Mould the pastry into a ball then roll out on a floured board or a very clean floured work surface. Also sprinkle a coating of flour onto the rolling pin. The flour is used to stop the pastry from sticking to the board and the pin.

Roll the pastry so that its area is big enough to cover the flan dish, then carefully place the pastry over the dish and mould it in the shape of the dish. Remove the edge of the overlapping pastry by running a knife along the rim of dish.

The next stage is to make the filling of the quiche.

N.B Before adding the filling to the pastry case it should be baked blind. This does not mean that you have to put on a blindfold and try find the oven. Baking blind is where a pastry case is pre-cooked in the oven for about 15 minutes. The pastry case has to be lined with dried lentils or dried peas. This stops the pastry from rising. If the pastry case is not baked blind there is a good chance that the pastry will be soggy.

Quiche Lorraine

The most famous quiche of all has to be the Lorraine. Its name derives from its region of origin, and is delicious eaten hot or cold.

Serves 4

Ingredients for filling

4 eggs
1/2 pint (300ml) of double cream
4 rashers of bacon
2 oz (50g) of cheese, optional
Salt
Pepper

Cut the bacon into small pieces, then fry lightly for a couple of minutes and place on the bottom of the pastry base. Beat the eggs together, add the cream, season and beat again. Pour over the bacon, sprinkle the cheese on top if required and bake in a hot oven Gas Mark 6 (425 Deg F, 220 Deg C), for 25 minutes or until the filling has set.

Alternative fillings can be used - try creating your own. This is another popular combination...

Cheese And Onion

Ingredients for filling

1 tbs of oil
4 eggs
1/2 pint (300ml) of milk
4 oz (100g) of grated cheddar cheese
1 onion, peeled and chopped
Salt
Pepper

Lightly fry the onions in the oil for a couple of minutes. Place the onion on the bottom of the pastry case. Beat the eggs together, add the milk, season and beat again. Pour over the onion, sprinkle the cheese on top, then bake in a hot oven on Gas Mark 6 (425 Deg F, 220 Deg C), for 25 minutes or until the filling is cooked.

Nachos

This is a quick and easy recipe that is perfect for any occasion.

Serves 4

Ingredients

2 tbs of oil
2 cloves of garlic, peeled and finely chopped
2 tsp of chilli powder
1 large onion, peeled and chopped
1 tin of chopped tomatoes (14oz)
1 large bag of tortilla chips
4 oz (100g) grated cheese
1 tbs of tomato purée
1 green pepper, deseeded and finely chopped
Salt
Pepper

Heat the oil in a large saucepan, then fry the onion and garlic for about 3 to 4 minutes. Add the chilli powder and the green pepper and cook for another couple of minutes. Then add the tomatoes, tomato purée and seasoning and cook for about 15 minutes. The sauce has to be well reduced otherwise it will make the chips soggy.

Whilst the sauce is cooking arrange the tortilla chips in a ceramic dish. When the sauce is ready, pour over the chips and finally cover with cheese. Then place under a hot grill until the cheese has melted - enjoy.

Spanish Omelette

As there are numerous variations on this meal, don't hold yourself back with what you add.

Serves 4

Ingredients

4 eggs
1 potato, cooked for 10 minutes and chopped
2 tomatoes, sliced
1 oz (25g) of peas
1 onion, peeled and chopped
Mixed herbs
Salt
Pepper

Beat the eggs, season, add the vegetables and pour into a flan dish. Bake at Gas Mark 6 (425 Deg F, 220 Deg C) for 15 to 20 minutes or until the mixture ceases to be runny. If you prefer the onions to be a little more cooked, fry them first for a few minutes.

Serve with a green salad.

Welsh Rarebit

Doesn't taste particularly Welsh, nor is it very rare.

Serves 1

Ingredients

6 oz (150g) of cheddar cheese
1/2 oz (15g) of butter
1/2 tsp of dry mustard
2 tbs of flour
2 slices of bread
4 rashers of streaky bacon

Grate the cheese and put into a small saucepan. Add the butter and mustard, then cook gently, stirring constantly, until the cheese has melted. Take the saucepan away from the heat and add the flour, beating it in until smooth. Allow to cool.

Grill the bacon and the bread, then spread the cheese mixture evenly over the toast. Grill until golden, then add the bacon and serve.

Pan Bagnat

Serves 1

Ingredients

1 very large roll
1 tbs olive oil
Wine vinegar
Sliced tomato
Tuna
Sliced egg
1 clove of garlic
Sliced cucumber
3 black olives
2 slices of green pepper
Salt
Pepper

Cut the roll in half and tear out some of the centre of the roll to allow room for the filling. Take the clove of garlic and cut in half then rub the inside of the roll with the cut edge. Pour a tablespoon of the oil over the inside of the roll. Fill the roll with the rest of the ingredients, pour the remaining oil evenly over, sprinkle a few drops of vinegar, season and put the top back on. Press down on the top of the roll with a degree of force to combine the flavours together. Do not serve immediately as it is best to wait a little while for the oil to penetrate the roll.

Best eaten sitting on the beach, with a cool beer.

Plain Omelette

Serves 1 to 2

Ingredients

1 oz (25g) of butter
2 or 3 eggs
A pinch of mixed herbs
Salt
Pepper

Beat the eggs together in a mixing bowl and add the seasoning. Melt the butter in a frying pan and pour in the eggs. As soon as the eggs start to cook lift up one edge of the omelette with a spatula, tilt the pan and let the uncooked egg run underneath. Continue to do this until the omelette is cooked, then flip it in half and serve on a warmed plate.

Cheese And Tomato Omelette

Serves 1 to 2

Ingredients

1 oz (25g) of butter
2 or 3 eggs
2 oz (50g) of grated cheese
1 chopped tomato
Salt
Pepper

Prepare as above, but add the cheese and tomato before adding to the frying pan.

Onion Omelette

Serves 1 to 2

Ingredients

1 oz (25g) of butter
2 or 3 eggs
1 medium sized onion, peeled and chopped.
Salt
Pepper

Melt the butter in a pan and fry the onions for a couple on minutes. Beat the eggs then add to the pan and cook as above.

Eggy Bread

Serves 2

Ingredients

3 eggs
4 tbs of milk
Slices of bread without the crusts
2 tbs of oil
Pepper

Beat the eggs and the milk together and season. Heat the oil in a frying pan. Dip a slice of bread in the egg mixture and then fry for a couple of minutes on each side.

Egg And Cheese Ramekins

Serves 1

Ingredients

2 oz (50g) of grated cheese
1 egg
1 tomato
Salt
Pepper

Grease a small ovenproof dish, preferably a ramekin dish or one that is about 3 inches (7.5cm) in diameter. Put grated cheese in the bottom of the dish and up the sides. Place in a slice of tomato and then the egg, trying not to break the yolk. Add the seasoning and cover with another slice of tomato and more grated cheese.

Bake in the oven for about 15 minutes at Gas Mark 4 (350 Deg F, 180 Deg C) or until the eggs are set.

Breakfast

The good old days when breakfast was a true meal appear to be long gone. Whereas breakfast used to consist of eggs, bacon, tomatoes, sausages, kippers and kedgeree, this daily dose of grease and lard has fallen from grace. A normal breakfast is now regarded as a slice of toast and a cup of coffee. Of course there are health risks associated with eating a plate of fried food everyday, but it sure tastes good.

If you are feeling in a romantic mood, then perhaps you could prepare breakfast in bed for your wife or partner. A tray with a small vase of flowers, a glass of orange juice and poached egg will probably give you a few welcome brownie points.

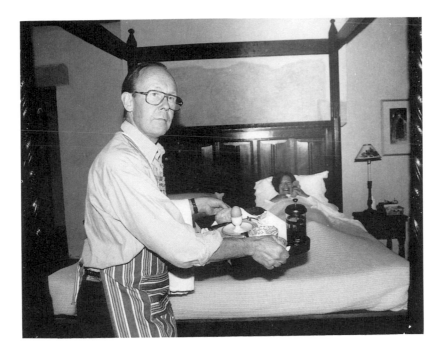

Cereal

If you want to eat a bowl of something not dissimilar to rabbit food for breakfast, fine. The first recorded incident of cereal crops being dunked in milk was in an industrial accident early in the 20th century. A farmhand had milked all the cows into a big bowl, ready for bottling, at the same time as his colleague had finished harvesting a field of Weetabix. The Weetabix was piled too high on a pallet, and toppled into the milk. At first they panicked, thinking all was wasted, but when a pig started to take an interest in the mixture, they realised that a new breakfast phenomenon had been discovered.

Cereals contain nearly all the nutrients needed each day. In fact, if you are stuck for food at any other time of day, you could do a lot worse than pour out another bowl of them.

If you normally pour spoonfuls of sugar onto cereal, try cutting down a little each day, and make up for the loss of flavour by adding some fresh fruit like apple, banana, strawberries or raspberries. If you don't have any fresh fruit add a handful of raisins.

Eggs

It has now been a few years since the egg scare, and I don't want to remind you of that nonsense. When choosing eggs there are a number of options. Battery farmed eggs account for the majority of egg production, but it is still possible to buy free-range eggs or barn eggs. Unfortunately, free range eggs are much more expensive than battery farmed eggs, but it is worth paying the extra as they have lovely deep coloured yolks and I believe they have more flavour due to the chicken's diet.

Many egg producers are now stamping a date on the egg. This is very sensible as it means you will no longer have to concern yourself with wondering how old that egg is that is sitting in the fridge. If you have an egg that is not stamped and you think it may be stale here is what to do. Break the egg onto a small plate. There are two indicators that the egg might be stale. The yolk will be flat and the two layers of egg white will have merged. If in doubt it is best to throw it away. This is a rule that should be adhered to with any food, especially meat if you think it might be past its best.

Scrambled Egg

Serves 2

Ingredients

3 eggs
1 oz (25g) of butter
4 tbs of milk
Pepper

Beat the eggs in a bowl and add the milk and pepper. Melt the butter in a saucepan and add the egg mixture. Stir the mixture as it thickens. Don't have the heat up too high, or else the egg will burn and stick to the pan.

Serve on top of hot buttered toast.

Poached Egg

Ingredients

1 egg per person
Butter or margarine

Put a nob of butter in one of the poacher rings, add the egg and cook for about 4 minutes, according to taste. There is a more traditional way of poaching eggs: Boil some water in a saucepan and the having broken an egg into a cup or mug slide it into the water. Only put one egg in at a time!

Fried Egg

Ingredients

1 egg
2 tbs of oil

Pour some oil in a frying pan, if you have a non-stick pan they are better. Don't let the fat get too hot, otherwise the egg will stick to the pan and bubble. Crack the egg on the side of the pan and plop the egg into the oil. Fry gently for about 3 minutes, basting occasionally. If you like your eggs American style (sunny side down), fry both sides of the egg.

Special Meals

There are plenty of good excuses for cooking a special meal. It could be a birthday, anniversary, Valentines day, or you just feel like it. Whatever the occasion a well cooked and imaginative meal will add to the memories. As with most of the recipes in this book, they are not particularly difficult, but remember there is so much more than just the cooking. Equally important is picking out a balanced menu. There is no point in serving 10 courses if you are going to be violently ill at the end of it. There is also no point in serving expensive food such as caviar or foie gras, if you don't really it. Cook what you and your partner enjoy eating. Choose good quality ingredients and give some consideration to the other 'romance factors'. If you go to all the trouble of cooking an elaborate meal, don't then spoil it by serving it with a can of lager and suggest that the meal is eaten on the sofa so that you can watch the football. This is unlikely to go down well! Choose a good bottle of wine, light a couple of candles, put on some subtle music and that's all you need.

Glazed Lamb Chops

The chops need to be marinated for several hours but they only take a few minutes to cook.

Serves 4

Ingredients

1 tbs oil
4 thick lamb chops
2 wine glasses of sherry
1 tbs mint sauce
2 tsp dark brown sugar
Salt
Pepper

Place the lamb chops in a bowl and mix all the ingredients together. Leave the chops in the marinade for at least 6 hours in the fridge.

To cook the chops take them out of the marinade. Heat the oil in a frying pan and fry the chops for a few minutes on each side. They should be served still pink in the middle.

When they are cooked, remove from the pan, pour in the remaining marinade and reduce by bringing to the boil. Pour the sauce over the chops and serve with fresh vegetables.

Pork And Cider Casserole

This is a recipe that was inspired by experimentation, however the end result is most pleasing.

Serves 4

Ingredients

2 tbs oil
1 large onion, peeled and chopped
2 cloves of garlic, peeled and finely chopped
1 tin of tomatoes (14oz)
1 tbs of tomato purée
2 tsp of herbes de Provence
1 green pepper, deseeded and chopped
1 courgette, sliced
4 pork chops
1 pint (600ml) of dry cider
1 mug of macaroni
1/2 mug of frozen peas
Salt
Pepper

Heat the oil in a large casserole dish, then fry the onion, garlic and green pepper for about 5 minutes. Then add the pork chops and fry on both sides for a couple of minutes. Add the tomatoes, purée, herbs, courgette, seasoning and cider then bring to the boil.

Simmer for about 40 minutes, adding the macaroni about 10 minutes before serving and the peas about 5 minutes after the pasta. Check to see if the macaroni is cooked before serving.

If the casserole begins to get a little dry add some water or more cider.

Caribbean Kebabs

Serves 4

Ingredients

1 1/2 lb (750g) of diced pork
10 rashers of streaky bacon
2 red peppers
3 bananas
1 large tin of pineapple rings

For the marinade:

4 tbs of golden syrup
6 tbs of soy sauce
6 tbs of pineapple juice
1 tbs of tomato purée
1 oz (25g) of fresh ginger
Pepper

Mix all the ingredients of the marinade together in a bowl, then place the pork in it and leave in the fridge for 6 hours or more.

Deseed the peppers and cut into 1 inch (2.5cm) pieces. Cut the bananas crossways into 1 inch (2.5cm) lengths and wrap each piece of banana in half a rasher of bacon. Cut the pineapple rings into 1 inch (2.5cm) sections.

Thread the above onto the skewers starting and ending with the red pepper. Thread the banana crossways to hold the bacon in place.

Baste with marinade then put in the oven at Gas Mark 7 (450 Deg F, 230 Deg C) for 20 to 30 minutes, basting regularly with any spare marinade.

Serve with rice.

Beef Stroganoff

Serves 4

Ingredients

1 lb (500g) of fillet steak
1 large onion, peeled and chopped
1 clove of garlic, peeled and finely chopped
4 oz (100g) of mushrooms, sliced
2 oz (50g) of butter
2 tbs brandy
1/2 pint (300ml) of soured cream
Salt
Pepper

Bash the steak with a rolling pin to flatten it out, but don't get too carried away. Cut into strips 1/2 inch (1.5cm) wide and 2 inches (2.5cm) long. Fry the steak in the butter for about 3 or 4 minutes, then remove from the pan and put in a bowl.

Fry the onions and garlic for 5 minutes, then add the mushrooms and cook until they have softened. Season and put the meat back in the pan. Cook for about 10 minutes, stirring occasionally to prevent burning.

Before serving, add the soured cream and the brandy and heat through. Do not allow to boil, otherwise the cream will curdle.

Steaks

The most popular steaks are rump, fillet, sirloin and entrecote. Fillet is the most tender and lean, but unfortunately the most expensive. Rump steak has a wonderful flavour but is not as tender.

Steaks are best grilled or fried:

To grill

Brush the steaks with butter and season with black pepper. Make sure the grill is hot before you cook the steaks. Grill each side for 3 to 4 minutes. If you want the steaks dripping with blood cook for slightly less time or eat raw. If you like your steaks well done cook for about 5 to 6 minutes on each side.

To fry

Heat a small amount of oil, preferably in a non-stick frying pan, wait till the pan gets very hot then put in the steak. Fry quickly for a couple of minutes to seal in the flavour. Turn down the heat, cook for 5 minutes for 'rare', 5 to 7 minutes for medium and 15 minutes for charcoal. Try to turn the steak over only once.

The above times for both grilling and frying will depend on the thickness of the steak.

Serve the steaks with fried potatoes, or new potatoes, a salad or fresh vegetables.

Marinated Chicken

Serves 4

Ingredients

2 tbs of oil
4 chicken breasts
Juice of 2 lemons
2 tbs of sherry or marsala
1 tsp of French mustard
Black pepper

This dish needs to be prepared a little in advance. If you don't have any sherry or marsala, it could be omitted.

Remove the skin from the chicken if it has not already been done. Dice the chicken breasts into bite sized pieces and put in a small mixing bowl along with the lemon juice, mustard, sherry and pepper. Mix well and leave in the fridge for several hours.

Heat the oil in a frying pan, then gently fry the chicken for about 10 minutes.

The chicken can be served with fresh vegetables of your choice and dauphinoise potatoes. See vegetables section for advice on preparing veg. If it is a special occasion why not try something different like mange-tout and dauphinoise potatoes.

Desserts

As a child it was the desserts that proved to be my weakness, anything with obscene amounts of chocolate and cream were shovelled down in amazing quantities. Those days of care free eating are now over, that unfortunate phenomenon when you stop growing taller and instead grow outwards has taken over.

Fresh Fruit Salad

Not even a hint of chocolate.

Serves 4

Ingredients

1 banana
2 oranges
1 apple
2 oz (50g) grapes
4 oz (100g) of strawberries
Juice of 1 lemon
2 tbs of sugar
1/2 pint (150ml) of water

The above ingredients are just a guide-line. You can use any fruit that is available or affordable. The given quantities will serve about 4 small bowls. If you are serving people rather than small bowls, the same quantities will do.

Wash all fruit before starting. Put the lemon juice and sugar in a mixing bowl and mix together.

Cut the apple into quarters, remove the core and chop into small pieces.

Peel the oranges using a sharp knife, making sure all the pips are removed. Cut into segments, cutting between the membranes.

Cut the grapes in half and remove the pips. Peel the banana and cut into slices.

Skin and quarter the pear, then core it and chop into small pieces. The strawberries should be hulled (that means remove the green bit at the top), and cut in half.

Put all the fruit in the bowl with the lemon juice, sugar, and water, and mix thoroughly.

Serve either on its own or with cream.

Pears In Red Wine

Serves 4

Ingredients

4 pears
4 oz (100g) sugar
1/4 pint (150ml) red wine
1/4 pint (150ml) water
Pinch of cinnamon
1 oz (25g) browned almond flakes

Put the wine, water, sugar and cinnamon in a large saucepan and heat gently until the sugar has dissolved.

Peel the pears trying not to damage the fruit, and leave the stalks on. Place the pears in the wine and simmer for about 20 minutes or until they are soft. When the pears are cooked remove from the pan and place in a serving dish. Reduce the wine sauce by boiling rapidly. It should become a syrupy consistency. Pour the wine over the pears and when cool, chill in the fridge. Before serving sprinkle with almonds and serve with cream.

Ricotta And Raspberry Crunch

A delicious summer pudding that does not have to be made with raspberries, you could use strawberries, bananas or grapes. Another alternative uses toasted pine-nuts instead of the almonds.

Serves 4

Ingredients

12 oz (300g) Ricotta cheese
8 oz (225g) fresh raspberries
Toasted almonds
Runny honey

Divide the ricotta into 4 bowls and arrange the raspberries around the edge of the cheese. Put about a tablespoon of honey on top of the cheese and then sprinkle with the toasted almonds. If you find that is a little bitter, either add more honey or dust with caster sugar.

Baked Apples

Serves 1

Ingredients

1 large cooking apple per person
Mincemeat
Brown sugar
Butter

Remove the cores from the apples and stand them in an ovenproof dish. Fill the hole in the apple with mincemeat and a teaspoon of brown sugar. Add a nob of butter on top. Put enough water in the dish to cover the bottom of the apples. Bake at Gas Mark 4 (350 Deg F, 180 Deg C) for about an hour.

After an hour test the apple with a skewer. It should be soft, but not too much. Serve with cream or ice cream.

Raspberry Brulée

Serves 4

Ingredients

8 oz (225g) of fresh raspberries
1/2 pint (300ml) of double cream or whipping cream
6 oz (150g) of demerara sugar or golden granulated

Place the raspberries in a shallow heatproof dish. Whip the cream until thick, (but not too stiff) and spread over the raspberries. Sprinkle sugar over the cream, covering it completely.

Pre-heat the grill and then place the brulée under the grill, until it is dark and bubbling. Remove from the grill and cool. Chill in the fridge for a couple of hours. A cheaper version could be made using sliced banana.

Poached Peaches

Serves 4

Ingredients

Tin of peach halves
1/2 oz (15g) of butter or margarine
2 tbs of brown or golden granulated sugar
1 tbs of brandy or whisky, optional

Drain the syrup from the peaches, reserving a small amount. Melt the butter in a saucepan. Add the peaches with the syrup and sugar.

Heat gently for about 5 minutes then stir in any brandy if desired.

If you have any flaked almonds or nuts, a few of these toasted and sprinkled on top taste good.

Croissant Pudding

Serves 4

Ingredients

5 croissants
1/2 pint (300ml) of milk
2 oz (50g) of castor sugar
2 egg yolks
2 oz (50g) of raisins
Vanilla Essence
Ground cinnamon
Brown sugar
Butter

Cut the croissants length ways and cut in half. Butter one side of the croissants and put to one side. Beat the egg yolks, caster sugar, milk, adding two drops of vanilla essence, then put aside. Grease an over proof dish and place a layer of croissants on the bottom, then sprinkle with raisins. Continue this until all the croissants are used up. Do not put too many raisins on the final layer as they are liable to burn.

Briefly beat the milk mixture, then pour over the croissants. Sprinkle with cinnamon. Leave to soak for at least 30 minutes.

Whilst the croissants are soaking preheat the oven to Gas Mark 4 (180 Deg C, 350 Deg F).

Sprinkle a thin layer of brown sugar over the top of the dish then place in the middle of the oven for 20 minutes. Remove from the oven, a add some more sugar and return to the oven for a further 20 minutes.

Biscuits And Cakes

The emphasis of this book is on preparing main meals rather than cakes and biscuits, as cooking main meals will be of more use. However, tea time comes round every afternoon, usually at about tea time, so an introduction to basic cake making is included. There is nothing fancy or difficult - I will leave that to others. Cake making is not easy. They can often fail to rise for no apparent reason, but you can't go too far wrong with a good old Victoria sponge.

Victoria Sponge

The Victoria sponge is easy to make and when still warm is hard to beat. As an alternative add cream between the layers.

Ingredients

4 oz (100g) of self-raising flour
4 oz (100g) of margarine
4 oz (100g) of caster sugar
2 eggs, beaten
Jam

(Two 7 inch/17cm sandwich tins are needed)

Mix together the sugar and margarine until they are smooth in texture. Gradually add the eggs to the mixture, then fold in the flour. Divide the mixture between the two baking tins (these need to be greased first, which means wiping the inside with a piece of greaseproof paper covered with fat). Make sure that the tops of the cakes are level, then bake in the oven for 20 minutes or so at Gas Mark 5 (400 Deg F, 200 Deg C).

The way to see if a cake is cooked is to stick a skewer or a clean dip-stick in the centre of the sponge. If bits of the mixture are stuck to it when it is drawn out, it needs to be cooked a little longer. If the skewer comes out clean, the cake is ready. If the dip-stick comes out below the minimum mark top up your oil.

Now turn the cakes out of the tins onto a wire rack (look in the grill pan for one). Once cooled, spread a layer of jam over one of the layers, sandwich the other one on top, and sprinkle with caster sugar.

Treacle Tart

This can be serve hot or cold, with cream or ice-cream or on its own. Ideal as a snack, a dessert or as cockney rhyming slang.

Serves 4

Ingredients

4 oz (100g) plain flour
2 oz (50g) fresh white breadcrumbs
3 tbs water
1 oz (25g) lard
1 oz (25g) butter
12 tbs golden syrup
2 tsp grated lemon rind
Salt

Add a pinch of salt to the flour and sieve. Cut the fat into small pieces and rub them into the flour until the mixture resembles fine breadcrumbs. Add a tablespoon of water at a time until a firm dough is produced. Cover a clean surface or pastry board with a sprinkling of flour. Roll out the pastry so that there is enough to cover the bottom and the sides of a 8 inch (20cm) flan dish. Mix the syrup, breadcrumbs and lemon juice together then spoon into the flan case.

Bake for about 25 minutes at Gas Mark 6 (425 Deg F, 220 Deg C), until golden.

Chocolate Crunch

Ingredients

4 oz (100g) digestive biscuits, crushed
4 oz (100g) rich tea biscuits, crushed
4 oz (100g) butter
3 oz (75g) golden syrup
1 oz (25g) cocoa powder
6 oz (100g) plain chocolate
Icing sugar

Using a piece of grease proof paper dabbed in butter, wipe the inside of a shallow baking tin. I know that using a can of WD40 would be quicker but it probably wouldn't taste as good. Melt the butter in a saucepan and add the syrup and cocoa, mix together then add the crushed biscuits. Remove from the heat. Stir the mixture thoroughly so that the biscuit crumbs are evenly coated. Transfer the biscuit mixture into the tin and press down the mixture using a back of a spoon and leave to cool.

To melt the chocolate place a Pyrex bowl on top of a pan of simmering water. Do not put too much water in the saucepan as there is a chance the water might boil over the edge. Place the chocolate in the bowl and let it melt. When the chocolate has completely melted remove the bowl from the heat using a pair of oven gloves and pour the chocolate over the biscuit mixture. Spread the chocolate so there is an even coating. Allow to cool then cut into squares or slices. Dust with icing sugar. If the weather is warm they can be kept in the fridge to stop them from melting.

N.B To crush the biscuits, put them in a clean bag, tie the ends and bash with a rolling pin.

Rock Buns

Ingredients

8 oz (225g) of self-raising flour
4 oz (100g) of margarine
3 oz (75g) of currants or raisins
A pinch of nutmeg
3 oz (75g) of sugar
1 egg, beaten
2 tbs of milk
A pinch of salt

Mix the flour, nutmeg and salt together. Then rub the flour and margarine together until they look like breadcrumbs. The next stage is to add the currants, sugar, egg and milk. The mixture should be fairly firm.

Grease a baking tray with some margarine. Mould the mixture into small lumps and place on the baking tray.

Bake for 15 to 20 minutes, Gas Mark 6 (425 Deg F, 220 Deg C).

Chocolate Cake

Ingredients

6 oz (150g) of self-raising flour
6 oz (150g) of margarine
6 oz (150g) of caster sugar
3 eggs
1 1/2 oz (40g) of cocoa
1 1/2 tbs of water

(For the icing)
8 oz (225g) of icing sugar
4 oz (100g) of plain cooking chocolate
1 1/2 oz (40g) of butter/margarine
2 tbs of warm water

Place the sugar and the margarine in a large mixing bowl and mix together, using either a wooden spoon or an electric mixer (which will save time). Add the eggs, one at a time.

In a separate bowl, mix the flour and the cocoa powder together, then add it to the creamed mixture. Continue mixing, adding water until a soft dropping consistency is achieved.

Divide the mixture equally between two 7 inch (17cm) sandwich tins. Bake in the oven at Gas Mark 5 (400 Deg F, 200 Deg C) for 25 to 30 minutes.

Test the cake with a skewer. If the mixture sticks to it, the cake needs a few more minutes in the oven.

When the cakes are ready, turn them out of their tins onto a wire rack (if available). Melt the chocolate by placing it in a basin and putting that over the top of a saucepan of boiling water. Be careful not to let the water boil over the top of the saucepan into the chocolate.

After the chocolate has melted, allow to cool. Cream together the butter and half the icing sugar, then add half the melted chocolate. Mix, and spread over one side of the cake, then 'sandwich' the two together.

The rest of the chocolate is used to make the icing on the top. Add the water and sugar to the chocolate, and spoon onto the top of the cake. Spread the icing around using a palette knife that has been dipped in hot water (this helps to spread the icing and stop it sticking to the knife).

The cake can be decorated with those little silver balls that break your teeth, or with tasteful designs of snooker tables etc.

Raspberry Buns

Ingredients

8 oz (225g) of self-raising flour
4 oz (100g) of caster sugar
3 oz (75g) of margarine
1 egg, beaten
1 tbs of milk
Raspberry jam
A pinch of salt

Rub the margarine and flour together using your fingertips, until the mixture resembles breadcrumbs. Add the sugar, salt, egg, and milk, and mix well. The mixture should be quite stiff.

Grease a baking tray, then shape the mixture into twelve balls and place on the tray. Make a little hole on the top and fill with a teaspoon of jam.

Bake in the oven on Gas Mark 7 (425 Deg F, 220 Deg C) for about 20 minutes.

Flapjacks

Ingredients

8 oz (225g) of porridge oats
4 oz (100g) of margarine
3 oz (75g) of sugar
4 tbs of golden syrup
A pinch of salt

Melt the margarine in a large saucepan, then add the syrup and leave over a low heat for a couple of minutes. Remove from the heat and add the sugar, salt and oats. Mix thoroughly using a wooden spoon, making sure all the oats are covered with syrup.

Grease a shallow baking tray and evenly spoon in the mixture. Cook for 20 to 30 minutes at Gas Mark 4 (350 Deg F, 180 Deg C). After cooking, cut the flapjacks into bars before they cool.

Scones

A cream tea, with thick scones oozing home-made jam and thick clotted cream, tastes as good as anything found in a French patisserie.

Ingredients

8 oz (225g) of self raising flour
2 oz (50g) of margarine
1/4 pint (150ml) of milk
A pinch of salt

Mix the flour and salt together. The flour is supposed to be sieved, but it's a bit time-consuming and doesn't make much difference anyway. Cut the margarine into small cubes and add them to the flour. Rub the mixture using your fingers, continuing until the result looks like breadcrumbs.

Add the milk and stir in using the blade of a knife to form a soft dough. Roll out the mixture on a floured board until it is about 1/2 an inch (1.5cm) thick. Cut into rounds using a biscuit cutter or a glass.

Grease a baking tray and place some scones on it, leaving enough gaps for them to rise. Brush some milk over the top of the scones to obtain a smooth and shiny finish.

Bake in the oven for 10 to 15 minutes at Gas Mark 7 (450 Deg F, 230 Deg C).

Cheese Scones

As for above, but stir in 4 oz (100g) of cheese before adding the milk.

Fruit scones

As for plain scones, but stir in 1 oz (25g) of sugar and 2 oz (50g) of dried fruit, sultanas, currants etc.

Batters

Yorkshire Pudding

Serves 4

Ingredients

4 oz (100g) of plain flour
1 egg, beaten
1/2 pint (300ml) of milk, or milk and water
Oil
A pinch of salt

Mix the salt and flour together in a mixing bowl, then make a 'well' in the flour and add the egg. Mix in the flour carefully, adding a little milk until all the flour is mixed in, then add the remaining milk. Beat the mixture for a few minutes until it is smooth. Pour a teaspoon of oil into the individual patty tins, then add 2 tablespoons of the mixture into each. Bake for about 15 minutes or until they have risen and browned.

Pancakes

Serves 4

Ingredients

4 oz (100g) of plain flour
1 egg
1/2 pint (300ml) of milk
A pinch of salt
Butter
Sugar (or any other topping)

Put the flour and salt in a bowl and add the egg into the middle. Pour in about a third of the milk. Stir gently, adding a little more milk in the process. Beat the mixture thoroughly, then add the rest of the milk. Stir well, then pour into a jug.

Melt a small piece of butter in a frying pan, then add a couple of tablespoons of the batter. Tip the frying pan to spread the mixture evenly. Fry until the underside is brown, then toss the pancake.

Scrape the mess resulting from the dropped pancake off the floor, then start again. This time, when the underside is brown, turn it over with a fish slice or a knife and cook the other side.

Tip the finished pancake onto a plate and cover with lemon juice and sugar.

Barbecues

There appears to have been a change in the weather over the last few years, mild winter's and hot summers are becoming the norm. Food is very much influenced by the seasons. A belly busting stew is the ideal companion for a cold winters night, whereas in the summer, salads and light meals are more appropriate. If the weather is warm eating outside is a must, (unless you live in a block of flats), so go al fresco and pretend you are on holiday.

At the first sign of fine weather all around the country barbecues are brought out from the garage and dusted down for the beginning of the barbecue season. Some may be a humble affair requiring kneeling down to turn the food over, others might be of a grander design. There are ones on trolleys, gas powered and those handcrafted out of a few bricks and a grill. There is something about having a barbecue that usually is regarded as a man's domain, in which he displays his vast skill at lighting the barbecue and turning over a few sausages, whilst holding a can of lager.

The Barbecue

When choosing a barbecue, think about how many people you are normally likely to cook for. It is no good trying to cook half a dozen steaks on a grill the size of a piece of toast: your guests will be waiting all night. Nor you do you want to have a monster of a barbecue if you are only going to cook a couple of shrimps once a year. However, it is always sensible to buy one that is too big rather than too small.

You tend to get what you pay for. The cheaper ones can be a little unstable and flimsy, so beware. The problem with buying a barbecue is they normally have to be assembled and there are often bits missing. If there is one on display ask if you can have that one! Some barbecues have covers that reflect the heat. This enables the barbecue to be used as a oven. I would personally recommend building one out of a few bricks and square grill. You don't need to be a DIY expert, and they are cheap and practical. Consult a DIY book for instructions on how to build one if you can't put one brick on top of another.

One last tip: I recently went to a barbecue party where the host had sensibly acquired half a oil drum, which is perfect for cooking large amounts. After a few minutes of lighting the barbecue it began to generate a little smoke, but as wood was being used not much notice was taken. However, five minutes later thick black smoke was billowing and as there was a breeze the guests were soon running to avoid the choking black smoke. The embarrassed host had failed to notice that the drum had a thin coating of tar inside which when hot produced a thick smoke and foul smell. The barbecue was abandoned and 40 guests waited in turn to use the grill!

Tip: If you are going to use an old oil drum, make sure that it is clean before use.

Barbecue Fuel

There are several choices. Charcoal is the most used fuel, and comes in two forms, briquettes or lumpwood. Either can be used. I have used wood and found it perfectly acceptable, just make sure the wood is not green. The advantage of briquettes is that they burn for roughly twice as long as the loose charcoal.

Lighting the barbecue

As this is regarded as a mans job it is taken very seriously, on par with lighting the Olympic flame. Women tend to find this display amusing, especially if it goes out. Perhaps this is why some men rather than risk the chance of the barbecue not lighting use half a gallon of lighter fuel just to make sure, and although it will normally light they usually lose a couple of eye-brows in the process.

Never use petrol or a similar fuel for lighting a barbecue as it is extremely hazardous. Use special barbecue lighter fuel or blocks. Alternatively use paper and kindling wood. I find that some of the lighter blocks can taint the food.

Once the barbecue is alight, the second stage of 'men taking the barbecue seriously' comes into force. This is almost as important as lighting it. Out come the foot pumps, hairdriers, and hot air guns to assist with getting the charcoal up to temperature. If you want to be really sad, don a snorkel and mask to keep the smoke out your eyes.

To get the barbecue up to cooking temperature will take about 40 minutes. The charcoal should be white before you begin to cook. How much charcoal you use depends on the size of the barbecue and how much food you have to cook on it. If you are cooking three courses you will obviously need more charcoal than if you are cooking only one course. If it is a party use plenty - it is embarrassing only having enough heat to cook half the food, so it is always better to use too much.

If when barbecuing you have too many flames, keep a bowl of water handy to douse them. Just flick some on the charcoal with your fingers. If you want to be clever, try using a small plant spray.

The Food

Cooking on a barbecue is more versatile than most people imagine, so apart from the usual burgers and sausages, try something new. Appetites always seem to grow during a barbecue, so make sure that you prepare enough food. Apart from the food prepared on the barbecue make plenty of salads and dips.

Lamb With Honey And Rosemary

Buy the thickest lamb chops available.

Serves 4

Ingredients

4 lamb chops
4 sprigs fresh rosemary
2 tbs runny honey

Pierce the lamb chops using a sharp knife and insert small pieces of rosemary. Put in a mixing bowl and spoon over the honey, so that the chops are evenly coated.

Place the chops on the barbecue and cook until the meat is cooked to your liking.

Marinated Chicken

Serves 4

Ingredients

4 plump chicken breasts
1 clove of garlic, peeled and finely chopped
2 tbs olive oil
1 tbs of herbes de Provence
Juice of one lemon
Salt
Pepper

Place the chicken breasts in a bowl the pour over the oil and lemon juice. Mix in the garlic, season, then sprinkle with the herbs. Put in the fridge for a couple of hours or longer if you have time.

When the barbecue is ready, cook each side of the chicken for 7-8 minutes. Check that the chicken is cooked all the way through before serving.

Vegetable Kebabs

Although meat is the preferred choice for cooking on a barbecue, vegetarians and pigs would probably disagree.

Serves 4

Ingredients

Olive oil
1 onion, peeled
1 red pepper, deseeded
1 yellow pepper, deseeded
4 tomatoes
1 courgette
12 mushrooms
Mixed herbs
Salt
Pepper

It really depends on the size of your skewers as to how many vegetables you use.

Prepare the vegetables by cutting them into chunks, then thread the vegetables onto the skewers, alternating between the different vegetables.

Place the kebabs on the barbecue and coat with olive oil and mixed herbs. When cooking the kebabs they need to be turned frequently to stop them burning. Season and serve with a salad.

Burgers

If you have not made your own before why not give it a go?

Serves 4

Ingredients

1 lb (500g) of minced beef
1 onion, peeled and finely chopped
2 oz (50g) of bread crumbs
1 tbs chopped fresh parsley
Dash of Worcester sauce
1 tbs olive oil
Salt
Pepper

Throw all the ingredients in a bowl, mix together using your hands, and divide the mixture into 4 portions. Shape each portion into something that resembles a burger. Cook for about 4 or 5 minutes on each side, or until brown. To produce a more exotic burger try adding chopped garlic and herbs.

Baked Bananas

Serves 1

Ingredients

1 banana
Brown or golden granulated sugar
Lemon juice

Peel the banana and place it on a piece of foil, shiny side uppermost, making sure the foil is large enough to wrap it up loosely. Squeeze the lemon juice over the banana, sprinkle with brown sugar, and loosely wrap up.

Place in the embers of the barbecue and cook until it is slightly soft to touch.

Serve with cream or ice cream.

Baked Bananas II

I have no doubt that if you not tried this recipe, after tasting it you will be smitten. Make sure that you use dark chocolate as milk chocolate is just not the same. (it's milkier and not as dark).

Serves 4

Ingredients

4 large bananas
4 oz (100g) dark chocolate

Take a sharp knife and make a sharp incision through the skin of the banana from end to end. Gently peel the skin apart and make another incision the length of the banana. Be careful not to pierce the other side of the skin. Break the chocolate into small pieces and then insert the chocolate in the cavity. Close the edges of the banana skin together, then wrap in a foil parcel. Place the bananas in the embers of the barbecue until they have softened and the chocolate has melted. Serve with thick double cream.

Entertaining

One of the most important reasons for being able to cook is to be able to entertain. Entertaining gives the ideal opportunity for demonstrating your new found skills, the combination of great food, copious quantities of wine and congenial company is a perfect mélange, the result should be pure unadulterated pleasure.

In theory, entertaining should be easy. You have learnt how to cook a simple yet elegant dish. You have chosen a good bottle of wine and you have gathered an interesting selection of friends together. The reality is that you burn the sauce, the wine is oxidised and undrinkable and you have to stop your guests from a political debate that is about to get messy. Oh yes, entertaining is such fun! When entertaining try to be prepared for any eventuality that you could possible imagine. If you have to invite a member of the anti vivisection society and a Frenchman who enjoys veal for breakfast, it might be prudent to seat them at opposite ends of the table.

The secret of successful entertaining is forward planning. If you don't plan you are likely to be heading for disaster. If you find entertaining something of a challenge, there are some basic rules that should be adhered to if you want to make it a less arduous task. As the host it is your responsibility for your guests' enjoyment. The host has to fulfil a number of roles: besides preparing and cooking the food, the host will have to look after the guests, make introductions, and keep the conversation going if it dries up.

Far too many people dislike entertaining because by the time the guests arrive they are exhausted and stressed after having slaved over a hot stove, only just finishing things off minutes before the guests arrive. You will feel flustered and certainly look flustered. It does not have to be this way. It is good to get into the habit of being so organised when entertaining that you can take the time to relax an hour before the guests arrive.

Planning Tips:

The Menu

This is a good place to start. If you serve good food you are on to a winner. However, there is no point in serving tantalising food if there is only enough for a small portion each. Obviously if you are serving something quite revolting they will be quite relieved, but in general make sure you cook enough, allowing for seconds. The same applies to the drinks. There can never be enough. Not wishing to encourage excessive drinking, I must admit that entertaining is usually more fun after a few bottles have been emptied.

Plan what you are going to cook well in advance and keep it simple. Don't try to be too adventurous: being over-ambitious is a recipe for disaster. It is sensible to try cooking a new recipe before the event, then you will have a idea if it will be suitable. You will know how long it takes to prepare and to cook as well as the level of competency required. If you don't try it out before hand, you increase the chance of it going horribly wrong. This would be embarrassing if it was an important occasion. It is often prudent to play it safe and stick to recipes that you know well.

Presentation

Food always looks and tastes better if an effort is made with the presentation. There is no point in going to a great deal of trouble to prepare a meal then serving it in an unappetising manner. Invest in a couple of attractive serving bowls and dishes, and a set of matching plates. If your cooking is less than palatable, if it at least looks attractive you might fool the recipient into thinking that it tastes OK.

● Make sure that all the plates, cutlery and glasses are clean. Eating off dirty plates will not make a meal appetising.

● The essence of presentation is to keep the food looking fresh and uncluttered. Plates should not be piled high with food - it makes the person feel obliged to clean their plate and if they have a small appetite this could be a struggle.

● Don't try to combine too many colours or flavours together, keep it simple and elegant.

● Don't forget to warm the plates and dishes before serving the food.

Wine

This chapter is only popping the cork on a subject that is incredibly fascinating and complex. The more I think about writing this chapter the harder it gets. There is so much that could go in, but this is a cookery book not a wine book so I'll try to keep it brief.

I believe in few rules when it comes to cooking and the same applies with wine. If you want to find out more about wine, then there are several excellent wine books available that can give all the answers. I would like to take this opportunity to thank Charles and Amanda Master of Masterwines who have been wonderful friends and have also given me the opportunity to further my interest in wine. They are both passionate about food and wine and their hospitality is unequalled. Many evenings have been spent in their home overlooking the Pyrenees, with us all in the kitchen, preparing food, eating food, talking about wine and drinking wine.

Having returned from the Vin Expo at Bordeaux, I am convinced that the wine trade is a truly satisfying profession. To be paid, for sampling wine all day sounds like heaven, and it appears that wherever there is wine you can be sure that food is not too far away. I was fortunate enough to accompany a friend, Philippe Busquets who kindly chaperoned me for three days. It was interesting to note that after a day of sampling wine, thousands of visitors got in their cars and drove home. There didn't appear to be a policeman in sight. Perhaps it is easier to turn a blind eye for the week rather than trying to work out the logistics of finding taxis for thousands of inebriated winies.

Wine consumption is on a upward curve and there seems little indication of a decline. There has also been a resurgence of wine production in many countries that had not produced wine on any great scale in the past. Undoubtedly the French still produce some of greatest wine in the world, their Bordeaux and Burgundies are unsurpassed. If you are looking for value then steer clear of the Bordeaux and the Burgundies and try regional wines. Areas of South West France, which include Minervois and Corbières, are producing very drinkable wines at sensible prices. However, there is no reason why you should stick to French wine. Try Italian, Australian, Chilean, Spanish, and American offerings. The only problem with the French is that they are so nationalistic they are reluctant to accept that any other countries are capable of producing wine of any merit. Attempting to track down an Australian Chardonnay in France is almost impossible: suggesting that they could possibly produce fine wine provokes disbelief. We are more fortunate in that it is possible to taste wines from virtually all areas of the world.

There are normally certain factors that dictate what wine we buy. Perhaps the most influential factor is price, with taste and availability coming into the equation. Most people purchase wine from an off-licence, supermarket or wine dealer. There is usually an excellent yet bewildering choice available, so where do you start?

It is important to have some knowledge about wine when choosing a bottle so you will gain some satisfaction from your choice. There is no point in picking up a bottle of sweet white if you only like dry wine. Unfortunately, most wine shops are reluctant to let you try before you buy. Tasting wine is one of the best ways of learning about wine, it is also a lot of fun.

Wine is generally available in three basic colours: red, white and rosé. To make wine is like a making a recipe, there are a number of basic ingredients, with the main ingredient being grapes. The other essential ingredients are sun, water, soil and climate. As in cooking when you repeat a recipe it will rarely taste the same twice, and the same applies with producing wine. The final taste of the wine will be determined according to how much rain, sun and frost occurred and the producer's skill. That is why there are good and bad years for wine. Usually the most crucial time for a producer is just before harvest, although science now plays an important role in the production of wine. The unpredictability of the weather can still cause problems, along with other natural disasters such as pestilence and disease.

Grapes

Vines are planted according to their surrounding, climate, and in many areas only certain grapes are allowed to be planted. There are some grapes that thrive in soils where a different type of grape would not survive, and this also applies to temperature. Each different grape variety has a recognisable characteristic that will ultimately decide on the type of wine produced. There are certain grape varieties that are used throughout the world and others that might only be found in a particular region. One of the most popular white wine grapes is Chardonnay, which is planted extensively throughout the world. However, a New Zealand Chardonnay will taste very different to an American or

French Chardonnay. This is why wine is such a fascinating subject. You can never get bored.

There are actually hundreds of varieties including several with unpronounceable names such as Gewurztraminer.

Here are a few of the more common grape varieties which are a little more pronounceable.

White Wine Grapes
The following are the most frequently used white grapes:

Chardonnay
Sauvignon
Semillon
Chenin Blanc
Muscadet
Riesling
Marsanne
Meursault

Red Wine Grapes
The following are the most frequently used red grapes.

Merlot
Cabernet Sauvignon
Cabernet Franc
Syrah (known as Shiraz in Australia)
Pinot Noir
Gamay
Grenache
Mouverdre

Wines are often produced from a blend of grape varieties. One of the frequent harmonies is between the Cabernet Sauvignon and the Merlot. In white wines Semillon is often mixed with Sauvignon Blanc. Beaujolais is produced from the Gamay grape which is ideally suited to the chalky soil of the region. Certain grapes such as Syrah produce wines that have a high degree of tannin which gives that tingling sensation on the gums and tongue. A high tannin content is needed if the wine is to be stored for a long period, but after a few years the tannin will mellow. A much softer wine is produced from the Merlot grape. After a while you will be able to choose wines that are to your taste when you know more about the traits of the different grapes.

To learn more about wine and why they are individual, the different grape varieties and their characteristics must be learnt. I haven't got room to describe these in this book so if you are keen, go out and by a wine book. Alternatively buy wines that are produced from different grape varieties and make your own notes.

Tasting Wine

Wine tasting is normally confined to a waiter in a restaurant asking if you want to try the wine. Here are a few wine tasting tips:

The waiter should only pour a small quantity of wine into the glass. This gives the wine more area to breath and the person who is about to taste the wine has a chance to swirl the wine in the glass to release some of the bouquet. In theory the glass should be held with thumb and the 2nd finger. Gently swirl the glass, but don't overdo do it, then tilt the glass and smell the wine. Take a sip, don't bother to try to gargle and make an exhibition. When in a restaurant it is inadvisable to spit the wine out!

Storing Wine

It is a shame that houses are now built without cellars: not only are they useful for storing all that unwanted junk, or hiding from the wife when she wants you to do yet another menial task, they are also the perfect places for storing wine. Wine, if it is going to be kept for long period of time, needs certain conditions or it will rapidly deteriorate. The more expensive the wine, the more care that should be taken.

If you do not have cellar: then other suitable places are under the stairs or in a spare room. It is essential that the temperature is kept constant. Try not to leave wine in a room where there are constant changes in temperature, ie in a centrally heated room that is in frequent use.

- The ideal temperature for storing wine is 55 Deg C, 12 Deg F.

- Keep the wine away from direct sunlight.

- Lay the wine flat so that the wine makes contact with the cork. This keeps the cork moist and stops it from drying out.

- Don't keep wine in a room that has strong odours as this can taint the wine.

- Try to leave the wine undisturbed.

Serving Wine

To get the most out of a bottle of wine it is important that it is served at the correct temperature.

Red Wine

Most red wines are served at room temperature which is supposed to be 16 Deg C, 65 Deg F. If your wine is cool don't be tempted to speed up the process by placing it near direct heat. Although as a rule red wines are served at the above temperature, there are a few wines that can benefit from being served at a lower temperature, even chilled, including some wines from the Loire valley, for instance St Nicholas de Bourguiel.

White Wine

White wine and rosé should be chilled before serving. For perfection there is an optimum temperature of 7 Deg C, 45 Deg F. To get a wine to temperature will take about two hours in the fridge, and about 30 minutes in an ice bucket. If you have an ice bucket make sure that you put plenty of water in with the ice.

Sparkling Wines

Personally I prefer sparkling wines, such as champagne, as cold as possible. There is something lacking in drinking warm champagne. Try to get the temperature down to about 5 Deg C - 40 Deg F. This does not mean the wine should be frozen.

Wine Glasses

If you want to get the most from your wine, it is important that you have the right glasses. In theory you should have two types of glass, one for the red wine and one for the white. A red wine glass has a wider body than a white wine glass, as red wine needs a greater area to allow it to breathe. When pouring red wine it should only be filled to two-thirds capacity, never fill a glass up to the brim as it doesn't allow the wine to breath and is awkward to drink.

A white wine glass should have a long stem so that there is no need to put your hand around the bowl of the glass which would warm it up. The bowl of the glass will be noticeably more slender than the red glass. This information is useful to know if you are eating out in a restaurant that has a plethora of glasses on the table.

Opening Wine

There is an increasing array of technical gadgetry for the opening of a bottle wine. The more complex they get the more expensive they are. For those who have a desire for gadgets to cover nearly all eventualities there is really is no need. The most important point to remember when opening wine is that the cork should be removed whole in a gentle manner that does not send wine shooting over your guests. I still use the most basic of corkscrews, the 'waiter's friend', as it is simple and effective. It also comes with a knife for removing the foil and can be used for removing bottle caps. The secret of using a waiter's friend is not to insert the corkscrew too deep into the cork. If it goes through the other side of the cork it is likely that small pieces of cork will fall into the wine. The idea behind the waiter's corkscrew is that side of the wine bottle is used as a lever. I have watched some people try to use a waiter's friend as a standard pull type corkscrew, but this doesn't work nearly so well.

Red Wine
There remains an element of disagreement as to whether red wine should be opened in advance of serving. Certain wines definitely require opening well in advance, such as magnums or wines with a high tannin content, others will not benefit.

Decanting
Wine that is kept for a number of years tends to develop a sediment that lies in the bottom of the bottle. This, of course, is disturbed when the bottle is opened and looks unsightly when entering a glass as well as tasting unpleasant. Before decantering make sure that the bottle has been standing upright for at least 24 hours and the decanter is clean. There is no point pouring wine into a decanter that has not been washed up and is covered in dust.

When pouring the wine into the decanter try to do it one go, keeping a smooth flow of wine. Keep an eye for any signs of any sediment beginning to rise up. By decantering you will inevitably lose a little wine that will have to stay in the bottom of the bottle.

Other Wine Tips:

Don't mix two different wines in the same glass. Always finish the first before starting a new wine.

Punches

Sangria

This famous Spanish punch is a real knockout, and is customarily drunk during the summer. A variety of fruit can be added according to personal preference. You will find that if you are drinking it in the sun after your third glass you would be ready to enter the bull ring.

Ingredients

2 bottles chilled red wine
4 tbs cognac
1 tbs caster sugar
3/4 pint (450ml) chilled soda water
Sliced peach
Sliced strawberries
Slices apple
12 ice cubes

Find large jug or bowl and place the fruit in the bottom. Pour the wine, cognac and sugar over the fruit and leave for an hour. Then pour in the soda and add the ice cubes.

Mulled Wine

Good after bonfire night or at Christmas.

Ingredients

1 bottle of red wine
4 to 6 tsp of sugar
The rind of 1 orange or lemon
2 inch stick of cinnamon
A blade of mace
2 cloves
Slices of orange/lemon for serving

Heat the wine and sugar, but do not allow to boil.
Then add the orange and spices. Strain and serve.

Index